insight text guide

Catriona Mills

Picnic at Hanging Rock

Joan Lindsay

Copyright © Insight Publications 2020

First published in 2020.

Insight Publications Pty Ltd
3/350 Charman Road
Cheltenham VIC 3192
Australia
Tel: +61 3 8571 4950
Fax: +61 3 8571 0257
Email: books@insightpublications.com.au

www.insightpublications.com.au

Copying for educational purposes
The Australian *Copyright Act 1968* (the Act) allows a maximum of one chapter or 10% of this book, whichever is the greater, to be copied by any educational institution for its educational purposes provided that the educational institution (or the body that administers it) has given a remuneration notice to Copyright Agency under the Act.

For details of the Copyright Agency licence for educational institutions contact:

Copyright Agency
Tel: +61 2 9394 7600
Fax: +61 2 9394 7601
www.copyright.com.au

Copying for other purposes
Except as permitted under the Act (for example, any fair dealing for the purposes of study, research, criticism or review) no part of this book may be reproduced, stored in a retrieval system, or transmitted in any form or by any means without prior written permission. All inquiries should be made to the publisher at the address above.

A catalogue record for this book is available from the National Library of Australia

Joan Lindsay's Picnic at Hanging Rock / Catriona Mills

Catriona Mills asserts the moral right to be identified as the author of this work.

ISBNs:
9781922378729 (print)
9781922378736 (digital)
9781922378743 (bundle: print + digital)

Cover design by Gisela Beer

Printed by Markono Print Media Pte Ltd

contents

CHARACTER MAP

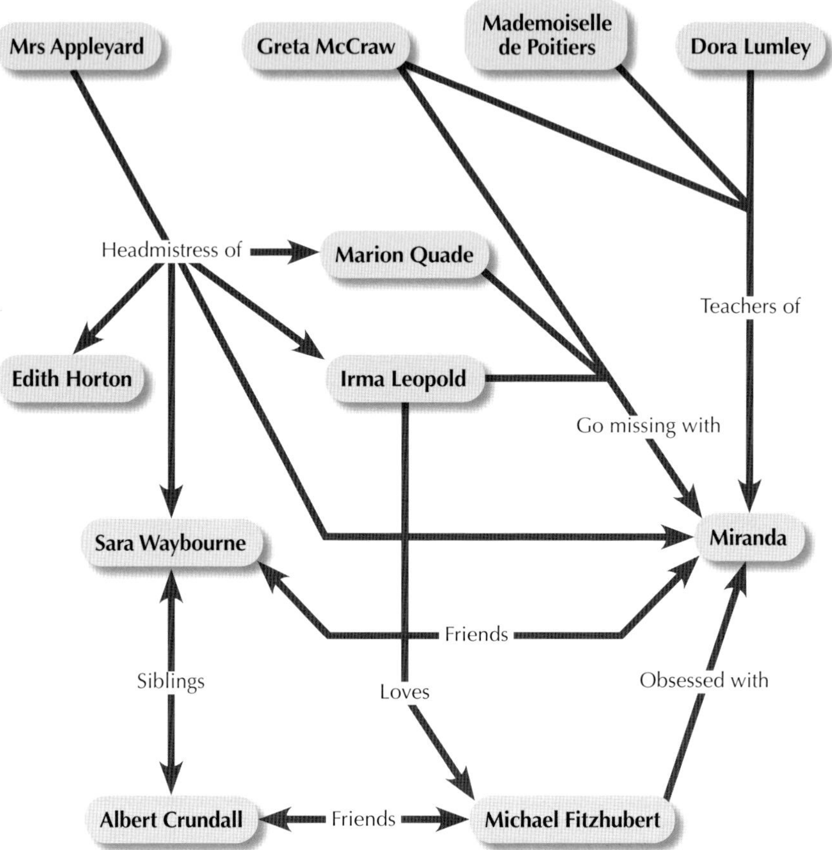

OVERVIEW

About the author

Joan Lindsay was born Joan Weigall in 1896 in St Kilda, Victoria, then a popular suburb among Melbourne's upper class. Her father, Sir Theyre Weigall, was a barrister and a Supreme Court judge. Her mother, Annie Hamilton, was the daughter of Sir Robert Hamilton, governor of Tasmania between 1887 and 1893: Sir Robert was Scottish and only lived in Australia for the period of his governorship.

Joan was educated at Clyde Girls Grammar School in St Kilda. After she left, the school relocated to the Mount Macedon region of Victoria, the setting of her fictional Appleyard College. Like Appleyard College, Clyde was a new school when Joan attended: she started at a local school called Carhue, which amalgamated with the newly founded Clyde in 1910. She likely drew on memories of this institution in *Picnic at Hanging Rock*.

After completing school, she had an ambition to become an architect, but her mathematics ability was not strong enough. Instead, she studied painting at the National Gallery of Victoria from 1916 to 1920 under painters including Frederick McCubbin, and set up a studio in Melbourne with fellow student Maie Ryan. She exhibited her work several times during this period.

She married Daryl Lindsay on Valentine's Day 1922, in London. Lindsay was a member of the famous artistic Lindsay family, and brother to well-known artists Lionel and Norman (author of *The Magic Pudding*) and lesser-known Percy and Ruby. Daryl Lindsay was also an artist – he and Joan had met as art students, and they held a joint exhibition after their marriage – but is best known as an arts administrator and critic. Joan and Daryl spent much of their married life at their estate, Mulberry Hill, on the Mornington Peninsula (which Lindsay described in her autobiography *Time without Clocks*), while Daryl Lindsay was director of the National Gallery of Victoria. Joan wrote *Picnic at Hanging Rock* at Mulberry Hill when she was nearly seventy years old.

Joan Lindsay is an author whose ongoing literary reputation rests on only one work. She published a relatively small number of works: occasional short stories and poetry, some plays, the autobiographies *Time without Clocks* (1962) and *Facts Soft and Hard* (1964), and her final work, the children's story *Syd Sixpence* (1982). She was also the author of *Through Darkest Pondelayo* (1936), a satirical novel in the form of a fictional travel book, which she published under a pseudonym. But none of these or her other works came close to attracting the same critical attention or reader devotion as *Picnic at Hanging Rock*.

First published in 1967, *Picnic at Hanging Rock* was made into a film in 1975 by Peter Weir. The film is considered one of the landmark works of Australian New Wave cinema. Both the novel and the film have had an indelible effect on people's understanding of Hanging Rock (a real place, Ngannelong) and the Mount Macedon region. The novel was also adapted for the stage by Tom Wright in 2016 and was adapted again as a six-episode prestige television series in 2018 (originally planned for broadcast in 2017, the fiftieth anniversary of the novel's publication).

Synopsis

The novel takes place across a period of roughly six weeks, from February to March 1900, with a coda set thirteen years later. On Valentine's Day in 1900, two teachers and their students from Appleyard College, a boarding school for young women in the Mount Macedon region of central Victoria, travel to nearby Hanging Rock for a picnic. The youngest pupil, Sara Waybourne, is left behind as a punishment for not memorising a set poem.

On the hot afternoon, four of the girls set out to climb the Rock, passing newly arrived Englishman Michael Fitzhubert and his uncle's coachman, Albert Crundall, on their way. Three of the girls disappear. The fourth returns to the group in a panic, and the group realise that one of their teachers is also missing. They arrive back at Appleyard College in an hysterical state. Despite searches with an Indigenous tracker and bloodhounds, the missing cannot be located. Michael Fitzhubert goes to search himself, and finds one of the girls, Irma Leopold, unconscious and only semi-clothed, but with no memory of what has happened. The others are never found.

As the weeks pass, the consequences of the events at the Rock stretch out. Irma Leopold falls in love with Michael Fitzhubert, but he is driven by an obsession with one of the missing girls, Miranda. Irma's father richly rewards Albert Crundall, who is able to leave his position as coachman and strike out on his own. Teacher Dora Lumley is dismissed from the college and dies, with her brother, in a hotel fire. And Mrs Appleyard, realising the mystery will affect her college's intake of pupils, becomes harsher and harsher with Sara Waybourne, an orphan whose guardian has not paid her fees for the term, until she drives her to her death. Sara's death is the final factor in Mrs Appleyard's downfall: realising her college is doomed, she makes her way to Hanging Rock, where a vision of Sara propels her over a precipice and to her death. A postscript in the form of a newspaper article describes the future of several characters and the college, and notes that the missing girls were never found.

A chapter describing the fates of the missing girls was removed from the book at the suggestion of Lindsay's editor, Sandra Forbes. In it, Lindsay suggests that the girls disappear into a hole in space, through a crack in the rock face; Irma, the last to reach the hole, is prevented when the hanging rock slowly tilts and blocks her way. The chapter remained unpublished until after Lindsay's death, when it appeared, with a collection of criticism, in *The Secret of Hanging Rock* (Lindsay 1987). Critics are largely in favour of the decision not to include the chapter, since an explanation of the events undercuts the Gothic mystery of the novel.

CHARACTER SUMMARIES

Major characters

These characters play a central role in the events of the text.

Miranda

The eldest of five children (and the only daughter) of a prosperous Queensland squatter family whose name is never given, Miranda is the popular head girl of Appleyard College, and the roommate of Sara Waybourne. She disappears on Hanging Rock, and her vanishing haunts the characters throughout the novel.

Irma Leopold

A popular, beautiful and extremely rich heiress, Irma goes missing on Hanging Rock, but is the only one of the three girls to be found. She falls in love with Michael Fitzhubert, but he is obsessed with Miranda. Her return is greeted with some suspicion by the other girls.

Mademoiselle Dianne de Poitiers (Mademoiselle)

A kind-natured, elegant woman in her early twenties who teaches dance and French conversation and oversees the girls' attire, Mademoiselle de Poitiers is particularly fond of Irma Leopold, and is kind to Sara Waybourne throughout Mrs Appleyard's mistreatment of her.

Michael Fitzhubert

An Englishman newly arrived in Australia and staying with his aunt and uncle, Michael is one of the last people to see the girls, and comes under some suspicion over their disappearance. He develops an obsession with Miranda, and must gently rebuff Irma Leopold.

Albert Crundall

Friend to Michael Fitzhubert and coachman to his uncle, Colonel Fitzhubert, Albert is one of the last people to see the missing girls, and also comes under some suspicion. He is Sara Waybourne's brother, although he does not realise that she is at Appleyard College.

Mrs Appleyard

A widowed Englishwoman who established Appleyard College six years before the fatal picnic, Mrs Appleyard, under pressure from the disappearances and worried about her public reputation, becomes dictatorial and vicious, especially towards Sara Waybourne.

Sara Waybourne

An orphan placed at Appleyard College by her guardian, Sara is one of the youngest students, and a thin, shy, sometimes sullen girl, fond of her roommate, Miranda. After the disappearances, she bears the brunt of Mrs Appleyard's anger. She is Albert Crundall's sister, although she does not realise he is in the Mount Macedon region.

Edith Horton

A younger student in the college, Edith is often described as unintelligent and overweight. She is the only one of the girls who returns from the Rock on the day of the disappearance.

Minor characters

These characters have some significance in the text, but are not explored in as much detail as the characters above.

Marion Quade

A mathematical prodigy and senior girl at Appleyard College, close friends with both Miranda and Irma, Marion is inclined to be dismissive of less intelligent students such as Edith. She goes missing on Hanging Rock.

Greta McCraw

A Scotswoman, the teacher at Appleyard College is a highly skilled mathematician. Uncomfortable in social situations, she places a high priority on propriety. She goes missing on Hanging Rock.

Dora Lumley

A governess at Appleyard College, Dora is unpopular with both pupils and colleagues. She has one brother, who works as a clerk in Warragul, 100 kilometres from Melbourne. Like Mrs Appleyard, she dislikes Sara Waybourne. She dies in a hotel fire with her brother.

Ben Hussey

Owner of the Mount Macedon livery stables, Mr Hussey drives the coach himself for important occasions, including the outing to Hanging Rock. He gives a detailed witness statement to police after the girls disappear.

BACKGROUND & CONTEXT

Lindsay wrote *Picnic at Hanging Rock* when she was sixty-nine years old. Her other novel, *Through Darkest Pondelayo,* had been published thirty years earlier: dedicated to the 'empire-builders', the satirical account of two English ladies on a 'cannibal island' is no longer widely read. When she wrote *Picnic at Hanging Rock* in 1966, she was living in Mulberry Hill, the home that she and Daryl had built in 1926, and had had to abandon briefly and rent out during the Great Depression, when their finances were poor. They returned to Mulberry Hill when their finances improved.

Picnic at Hanging Rock was said to have been inspired by a dream, a form of inspiration often connected with the Gothic novel: *Frankenstein* (1818), *The Strange Case of Dr Jekyll and Mr Hyde* (1886) and *Dracula* (1897) – three of the most iconic Gothic stories – were all said to have been inspired by dreams. The story of the dreaming of *Picnic at Hanging Rock* was told by the Lindsays' long-term housekeeper, Rae Clements: Janelle McCulloch, in *Beyond the Rock* (2017), recounts Clements' version of the novel's writing, which includes not only the first dream but also, seemingly, dreams on each subsequent night as the novel was being written (McCulloch 2017, pp.143–5). According to Clements, 'She would come down from her study each day and say she'd had the dream again. Then she would discuss the characters and what they were up to' (McCulloch 2017, p.144). Lindsay's own account is rather more ambiguous: she told her literary agent that 'I just sort of thought about it all night and in the morning I would go straight up and sit on the floor, papers all around me, and just write like a demon!' (McCulloch, p.144). Clements' account suggests a series of dreams, while Lindsay's suggests a dream followed by wakeful thinking and planning. Whichever is more accurate, the account of the instigating dream is part of the mythos of *Picnic at Hanging Rock*. Dream-inspiration may be part of a myth-making process that gives an impression of inspiration being supernaturally bestowed on the author; combined with Lindsay's presentation of the novel as possibly factual, this has an unsettling effect on the reader, disrupting our sense of a novel as a fictional work created consciously by the author. Certainly, it is a dreamy narrative, in which characters unexpectedly fall asleep or wake 'from uneasy sleep' (p.129), spend long periods unconscious, hallucinate and move through the day with a 'drooping, dream-heavy head' (p.166).

Picnic at Hanging Rock is set in 1900, the period of Joan Lindsay's early childhood, and just before Australia achieves Federation, bringing the six self-governing colonies together under a federal government. The novel recreates a sense of the leisured world of the rich in the period before World War I: doctors, lawyers, politicians and retired army colonels spending the cooler months in the sophisticated city of Melbourne, and the warmer months among the slopes of Mount Macedon, in large houses supported by an army of servants to care for their horses, tend their expansive grounds, and cater to tennis and garden parties. Barring the inversion of the seasons for a hot February, it is, in many ways, a world imported directly from England – hence Irma, who has travelled across the world, fits into it quite naturally, while Michael, who has turned his back on England, chafes at its restrictions. It is a world of white dresses and blue ribbons, gloves and hats, picnics and valentines. But it is also a world where doting parents might not hear of their only daughter's disappearance until weeks afterwards, where a wealthy man can adopt a friendless orphan and where a teacher can have absolute power. By 1967, when *Picnic at Hanging Rock* was published, this world must have seemed as dreamlike to readers as the novel itself.

Despite its Edwardian setting, *Picnic at Hanging Rock* was published at a moment of social change in Australia. The White Australia policy, which had restricted immigration by people of non-European backgrounds since 1901, had been slowly relaxed since the end of World War II, and Harold Holt's government, elected in January 1966, effectively ended it as official government policy. Australia had also committed its support to the Vietnam War, which would run from the mid-1950s to the mid-1970s. In 1967, an Australian referendum changed the way in which Aboriginal Australians were counted in the census and altered federal governance around Aboriginal affairs, marking a key moment in increasing Aboriginal activism and helping pave the way for significant changes in areas such as land rights. The dream world of Edwardian Australia had changed permanently.

Simultaneously, Australian fiction was entering into a significant period, during which some of the country's best-known novels would be written. For example, Patrick White, Australia's only winner of the Nobel Prize for Literature, published his best-known works at this time (beginning with *Voss* in 1957), although he had been writing since the 1930s. Novels of this period, like *Picnic at Hanging Rock,* looked to the Australian landscape, lifestyle and history for their inspiration: the period also saw significant works by Randolph Stow *(To the Islands,* 1958), George Johnston (*My Brother Jack,* 1964), Dymphna Cusack and Florence James (*Come in Spinner,* 1951) and Nevil Shute (*A Town Like Alice,* 1950), among others. All these works contributed to a new sense of Australia as a legitimate site for creative work – no longer an isolated outpost of the British Empire, but a thriving and unique country with its own culture. In a sense, Michael Fitzhubert's increasing embrace of Australia in *Picnic at Hanging Rock* is a reflection of this broader process.

Reception

Picnic at Hanging Rock was published by Cheshire in Melbourne in 1967; an English edition was released in 1968 and an American edition in 1970. It was somewhat superficially but positively reviewed on its Australian publication, including in *The Bulletin,* then one of Australia's most influential literary magazines, and in *Walkabout,* a popular travel publication. But its enormous influence on Australian literature and culture is due in no small part to the critically lauded film directed by Peter Weir, released in 1975.

During the 1970s, Australian film, which had flourished in the silent era of the early twentieth century but languished since the 1950s, was beginning to enter into a period now called the Australian New Wave. Films of the New Wave focused strongly on the Australian landscape; they included Nicolas Roeg's *Walkabout* (1971) and Ted Kotcheff's adaptation of another Australian Gothic classic, *Wake in Fright* (1971).

Picnic at Hanging Rock – with its hot and hallucinogenic landscapes, ethereal girls in white and unexplained central mystery – became emblematic of this period of filmmaking. According to Film Victoria, it made over $5 million at the box office, which was a staggering amount in the mid-1970s – particularly when Australian cinema was just emerging from a long hiatus in the 1950s and 1960s. It was also successful internationally, including winning a BAFTA (British Academy Film and Television Award) for cinematography. It remains an Australian classic, and continues to drive interest in the novel, which has been republished at least fifteen times since the film's release, and translated into French, Italian, Polish, German, Spanish, Danish, Japanese and Slovenian.

Miranda – the most popular and the most elusive of the characters – remains a significant figure: the visitors' centre at Hanging Rock, for example, includes a sculpture of Miranda posed among the rocks. There has been some suggestion in recent years that Miranda's popularity helps obscure the pre-colonial significance of Hanging Rock: in 2017, the fiftieth anniversary of the novel's publication, Amy Spiers, a PhD student at the University of Melbourne, launched Miranda Must Go, a 'counter-memorial action' that drew attention to the relative importance placed on the fictional Miranda over the reality of colonial displacement and violence. The campaign asserted that a missing imaginary girl was less significant to the site than the removal of the traditional owners. Similarly, conceptual artists Dominique and Dan Angeloro (who work as Soda_Jerk) reference *Picnic at Hanging Rock* in their video artwork *Terror Nullius* (also 2017), which, as the name suggests, addresses some of the ways in which colonial history denies its own violence.

Fact or fiction?

Lindsay opens *Picnic at Hanging Rock* with a remarkable author's note:

> Whether *Picnic at Hanging Rock* is fact or fiction, my readers must decide for themselves. As the fateful picnic took place in the year nineteen hundred, and all the characters who appear in this book are long since dead, it hardly seems important.

This insistence that the reader must decide whether the novel is fact or fiction creates a sense of mystery around it, and plays into its dreamlike, hallucinogenic quality.

The myth-making around the novel's veracity began soon after publication. For example, a brief review in *The Bulletin* opens with the claim, 'A friend in Victoria assures me the school of the mystery is well known. Certain other fairly minor matters, people and places are actual, and Hanging Rock is a tourist attraction' (*The Bulletin* 1967, p.82).

This sense that the novel might be true has continued to linger, and readers sometimes seek to trace its origins to some experience in Lindsay's life. Janelle McCulloch's *Beyond the Rock* (2017), for example, suggests that a picnic at Hanging Rock when Lindsay was four years old may have been the impetus; as evidence, she draws on interviews with Martin Sharp, who was a creative consultant on the 1975 film. Even now, some fan sites on the internet will insist on the story's veracity, despite there being no evidence of a real Appleyard College or missing students. However, these speculations can only ever be myth-making, since Lindsay, as her author's note indicates, preferred to leave the matter open-ended.

GENRE, STRUCTURE & LANGUAGE

Genre

Picnic at Hanging Rock draws on a genre that would have been familiar to readers in the 1960s: the school story. With roots reaching back to didactic tales of the eighteenth century, the school story reached its familiar form in the mid-nineteenth century and remained relatively unchanged for a century: Enid Blyton's popular *Malory Towers* and *St Clare* stories, published in the 1940s and 1950s, are actually relatively late additions to the genre, and it continues today in series such as the *Harry Potter* and *Vampire Academy* books. The traditional school story involved the arrival of a new girl at an established (usually boarding) school and the exploration of the rules, lessons, sporting events and often conflicts, such as bullying or cheating, she endured. In nineteenth- or early twentieth-century examples, the trope (motif) of a girl arriving at an English boarding school from the 'colonies' (generally Australia or New Zealand) sometimes appears: the new girl would initially be more casual in her manners than her English counterparts, but often surprisingly good at sports, especially cricket. *Picnic at Hanging Rock* draws on some of the familiar tropes of girls' school stories: the close community, the bullying, the groups of popular and unpopular students and teachers. Rather than the usual realist school story, however, Lindsay injects her tale with Gothic elements.

Like school stories, the Gothic started in the eighteenth century, with Horace Walpole's publication of a slim novel called *The Castle of Otranto* (1764), which was rich with ominous prophecies, predatory aristocrats and an inexplicable giant helmet. The term 'Gothic' comes from a form of art and architecture popular in the medieval period. But as other authors followed Walpole's example, the term 'Gothic fiction' took hold, and came to describe literature that evokes horror or terror in its readers. Horror is usually understood as the feeling that follows a frightening sight or experience, whereas terror is the sense of dread and anticipation that precedes it. In *Picnic at Hanging Rock*, for example, the final appearance of Sara Waybourne is a moment of horror, whereas Edith's apprehension as she approaches the Rock is a moment of terror.

The Gothic explores horror and terror through engagement with the concepts of the uncanny, the supernatural and the sublime. 'The uncanny' is a way of describing a moment where something strangely familiar becomes unsettling or mysterious. Psychoanalyst Sigmund Freud (1856–1939), author of an influential essay on the uncanny, used lifelike dolls as an example. In *Picnic at Hanging Rock*, the instant when the girls turn their backs on Edith and walk up the Rock is an uncanny moment. 'The supernatural' refers to any event outside scientific understanding, such as the disappearances of the girls or Irma's mysterious reappearance. 'The sublime' is a quality of greatness beyond human ability to calculate or describe – something that 'takes us beyond ourselves'. The sublime can be present in anything from the physical to the moral, but in Gothic literature is often centred on the landscape. Since the first Gothic novels were usually set in Europe, they generally drew on the vast landscapes of the Swiss Alps or the rich cultural and architectural history of Italy or Eastern Europe for the evocation of the sublime. In *Picnic at Hanging Rock*, the Rock itself is the key example of the sublime, and is indicative of the sublime's ability to unsettle (particularly Edith) as well as uplift.

Although based on these classical models of the Gothic, Lindsay's particular mode of Gothic writing is known as Australian Gothic. Drawing from its literary predecessors in its use of horror and terror, in its hints of the supernatural and in the strong presence of the uncanny, Australian Gothic moves away from the European and the medieval. Instead, it presents a silent, menacing landscape, vast spaces of bush or desert that could swallow people without a trace. Such depictions of Australia focus on the position of the settlers within this space: Eva Reuschmann, discussing the Gothic in Australian film, suggests that 'landscape functions not only as a cultural icon of national identity but as a psychological frame for women's entrapment in a colonial society' (Reuschmann 2004, p.9), while Gerry Turcotte argues that Australian Gothic works to reinforce the colonial space as a site of disruption, and 'encapsulate[s] perfectly the tensions of New World settlement and subsequent displacements, ruptures and contestations of the national "form"' (Turcotte 2017, p.206). In *Picnic at Hanging Rock*, Lindsay juxtaposes the Edwardian setting with the ancient bushlands and rock formations to create a specifically Australian sense of the uncanny, in what became a pioneering example of the Australian Gothic. But she is also drawing on older modes of Australian writing.

Australian writing has a long tradition of 'lost in the bush' narratives: the wide Australian landscape – which, to the colonists, appeared to be uninhabited and uncultivated – was often presented as swallowing children and sometimes adults whole. One of the earliest and most persistent examples was the three Duff children, who in 1864 were missing for nine days before being located by Indigenous trackers. The children were the subject of multiple poems and stories aimed at young readers, most of which had a moral lesson. The disappearance of the three schoolgirls and their teacher – especially since it is unexplained – draws from these persistent stories. As discussed in 'Background & context', this is sometimes seen as a problematic aspect of the novel, since it omits the significant displacement of the traditional owners.

Structure

Picnic at Hanging Rock takes place over roughly six weeks in early 1900: it begins on St Valentine's Day, 14 February, and ends on 26 March. The narrative marks the beginning date with cards, a heart-shaped cake and Miranda's toast to St Valentine on the way to the picnic. The end date is marked by the girls' countdown to the Easter holidays: the boarders leave Appleyard College on 25 March (p.223), and it is the next day that Sara's body is found. This structure reveals Lindsay's obsession with time in the novel: although time occasionally slows or resists measurement at key moments in the text, it nevertheless moves relentlessly on all the while.

Picnic at Hanging Rock regularly interweaves documents into the story: letters, telegrams, statements to the police and newspaper articles. These items counterbalance the third-person narrative (see below) by offering an alternative point of view: for example, Mr Leopold's anxiety about his daughter is conveyed more effectively in the brusqueness of a telegram (p.133) than it would be by the narrator's description. Such interpellated documents are also sometimes used to give a sense of verisimilitude, or credibility, to a fictional narrative: the inclusion of a newspaper article, for example, gently suggests that the story might, in fact, be a real event.

The interweaving of documents is common in Gothic fiction: Horace Walpole's *The Castle of Otranto* (1764), the first Gothic novel, masquerades as a medieval manuscript, and Ann Radcliffe's novels, the archetypal classical Gothic texts, usually include the heroine finding a manuscript that reveals important details. As a much later example of the Gothic, Bram Stoker's *Dracula* (1897) is told entirely in a collection of diary entries, letters and newspaper articles (called an epistolary novel). The more uncanny a story, the more its drama can be heightened by this technique.

Narrative point of view

Picnic at Hanging Rock uses a deceptively simple third-person narrative point of view, in which an unseen narrator relates the events of the story, including the inner thoughts of the characters (in contrast to a first-person work, which is narrated by a single character and limited to their perspective). Third-person narration can be limited, showing the interiority of only one characters or a small group, or it can be omniscient, letting readers into the heads of every character.

The third-person narration in *Picnic at Hanging Rock* is usually limited. At times, the narrator shows an intimate knowledge of the characters' thoughts: for example, when Mademoiselle is thinking of her fiancé during the picnic (p.28). But the narrator never allows the reader to see inside Miranda's mind; she is only ever described through the thoughts of other characters, so that she remains as much an enigma to us as she does to Michael and others in the novel. Furthermore, the narrator often uses terms or descriptions that are clearly the words of the characters, not of an omniscient narrator: for example, when the narrator calls Mademoiselle 'the impertinent hussy' (p.217), the expression clearly belongs to Mrs Appleyard but is presented in the voice of the narrator. In this sense, the third-person narration is sometimes omniscient and wide-ranging, and sometimes tightly focused in the consciousness of a single character. Like other aspects of the novel, this unbalances the reader, who is never entirely certain what mysteries will be revealed to them.

CHAPTER-BY-CHAPTER ANALYSIS

Chapter 1 (pp.5–22)

Summary: *Appleyard College, and its headmistress, staff and students, are introduced; the students, except Sara Waybourne, set out with two teachers for a summer picnic at Hanging Rock.*

The hydrangeas, which the gardener is watering in the opening description of the college, are the ones among which Sara Waybourne's body is belatedly found at the end of the novel. This is one of several images, including the Axminster carpets, that are picked up again in the final chapter of the novel. The opening descriptions emphasise the bright, sunny, warm weather, which is counter to a classical Gothic novel, but which Lindsay manipulates into a dreamy, hallucinogenic Australian Gothic.

The emphasis on time, which becomes more marked in Chapter 2, begins here, as coach driver Mr Hussey checks the sun rather than his watch, in a sequence where the landscape is so still as to be almost frozen in time (p.19). Furthermore, the passage from the road through the gateway into Hanging Rock Picnic Grounds is described as a journey 'out of the known dependable present and into the unknown future' (p.22): Lindsay is referring in part to the coming tragedy but also foreshadowing the strange movement of time in and around Hanging Rock.

Key vocabulary

Axminster: a town in Devon, where a carpet-making technique originated, producing high-quality carpets with colourful, complex designs.

Caryatids: stone carvings of female figures used as pillars.

Pompadour: a hairstyle originating in seventeenth-century France, which became popular again in the 1890s.

White elephant: an object whose possession and maintenance costs are out of proportion to its value or use. The phrase 'white elephant' can also imply that the owner is not free to get rid of the object.

'Wreck of the Hesperus': a narrative poem by American Henry Wadsworth Longfellow, published in the 1840s and popular as a recitation piece because of its ballad style.

Q Given the novel's obsession with time, what is the significance in Mademoiselle de Poitiers marrying a horologist (clockmaker)?

Q How does this chapter set the mood and tone of the novel?

Chapter 2 (pp.23–34)

Summary: *Mademoiselle and the students drowse; Miranda, Irma, Marion and Edith explore the Rock, passing Michael Fitzhubert and Albert Crundall.*

This chapter emphasises the barriers placed between society and nature: the girls have slowly been stripping away the markers of polite society – first their gloves (p.17), then their hats (p.18) – although Mrs Appleyard only permitted them to remove their gloves (p.13). The sequence on pages 24–5 emphasises the remaining physical barriers, which prefigures the slow removal of even these trappings.

- The girls climbing Hanging Rock remove their stockings and boots.
- Irma returns without her corset.
- Greta McCraw moves through the bush in only her drawers, over which she would have been wearing not only a dress, but also a petticoat.

Mrs Appleyard's later loss of control is marked in a similar way: as she creeps out at night to see whether Sara's room contains anything incriminating, she appears as an 'old woman ... with pendulous breasts and sagging stomach': 'No human being – not even [her late husband] Arthur – had ever seen her thus, without the battledress of steel and whalebone' (p.226).

This chapter also develops the theme of the slowing and stopping of time, hinted at in the previous chapter. Lindsay was fascinated with time and its measurements throughout her life: her autobiography was called *Time without Clocks*, as she and her husband apparently did not keep clocks in their home. In this chapter (pp.26–7), various characters find that their watches have stopped (Mr Hussey and Miss McCraw) or they are not carrying the one they normally would (Mademoiselle). Most striking is Miranda, who has stopped wearing her 'pretty little diamond watch' because, she says, 'I can't stand hearing it ticking all day long just above my heart' (p.27), as though the movement of time (a human construct, marked by the watch) is counter to the natural rhythms of the heart.

Key vocabulary

Botticelli: Sandro Botticelli (c.1445–1510), a Renaissance painter best known for his religious artworks.

Devil's Island: an infamously brutal French penal colony in French Guiana. French army captain Alfred Dreyfus was imprisoned there in 1895, wrongly convicted of passing military secrets to the Germans. 'The Dreyfus affair' was a major political scandal that divided French society and likely made an impression on teenage Michael.

Gold repeater: a watch that chimes the hours and minutes at the press of a button.

Sèvres: the Manufacture national de Sèvres has been renowned for its production of fine porcelain since the eighteenth century. Mademoiselle's clock is likely a small ('carriage') clock with porcelain panels.

Solar topee: also given as 'sola topee', this is another name for a pith helmet, a light-coloured, cloth-covered helmet issued to European military personnel serving in tropical climates. The Colonel, as this and other hints suggest, saw service in India.

Uffizi: a famous art gallery in Florence, Italy.

Q How do Marion's plans to 'measure' the Rock run counter to the idea of the sublime in Gothic fiction?

Q This chapter establishes Michael's character. How does he change across the novel?

Key point

Although she is a minor character, Greta McCraw is an interesting example of the novel's interrogation of social mores. She is more concerned than Mademoiselle with the social parameters that mark the boundaries beyond which well-brought-up girls cannot pass: for example, she only removes her gloves – stripped off by everyone else during the long, hot journey, with Mrs Appleyard's permission – when she 'had absently begun to eat a banana with disastrous results' (p.25).

Chapter 3 (pp.35–44)

Summary: *The four girls continue to climb Hanging Rock.*

This chapter contains a sustained account of the concept of the sublime, centred particularly in the description of the Rock on pages 35–7. The Rock is presented as both free from human occupation (p.37) and capable of obliterating any signs of passage (p.36): both of these prefigure the fruitless search for the girls after their disappearance.

The moment at which the girls, led by Miranda, walk away from Edith and disappear is an example of the uncanny, a key element of Gothic writing (see 'Genre, structure & language'): the girls are described as 'sliding over the stones on their bare feet as if they were on a drawing-room carpet' (p.44). The idea of the landscape in contrast to the colonial domestic spaces will recur as Mrs Appleyard makes her way up to the Rock at the end of the novel: 'at last, after a lifetime of linoleum and asphalt and Axminster carpets, the heavy flat-footed woman trod the springing earth' (p.243).

Key vocabulary

Covent Garden: the Royal Opera House, located in the Covent Garden district of London, is known as 'Covent Garden'.

'At the Hanging Rock': this painting by William Ford is held at the National Gallery of Victoria, where Daryl Lindsay was director from 1942 to 1956.

'The boy stood on the burning deck': a line from 'Casabianca' by Felicia Hemans, a poem taught in many schools at the time and thought to portray the ideal of courage.

Q How crucial do you think the idea of the uncanny is to the novel?

Q What is the significance of the strange sleep into which the girls fall?

Chapter 4 (pp.45–57)

Summary: *The picnickers return to the college with news that the girls and Miss McCraw are missing.*

This chapter contains the first of a series of interpellated first-person narratives, which appear throughout the novel (see 'Genre, structure & language').

It also reveals the character of Mrs Appleyard in more detail: she appears in passing (distant and majestic on the balcony) in Chapter 1, but becomes of greater significance from this point on in the novel, and this chapter gives the reader an intimate perspective on her motivations through a dream of her late husband and her complacent thoughts on Appleyard College's success (soon to be in ruins).

The reader also sees her first direct engagement with Sara Waybourne: characters in Chapter 1 hint that Mrs Appleyard might be rather strict with Sara (p.12), but the encounter in the schoolroom (pp.46–7) is the first exchange between them the reader sees. This relationship will be the driving force of the rest of the novel.

The return of the girls – 'all hatless, dishevelled, incoherent' (p.52) – is the first of several significant moments of hysteria in the novel, including when Irma's return is announced and the sequence in the gymnasium.

Key vocabulary

'If you are really watching the sparrows fall as it says in the Bible': a reference to Matthew 10:29: 'Are not two sparrows sold for a farthing? And not one of them falls to the ground apart from your Father's will.'

Miss Milligan: a form of Patience, a single-player card game, played with two decks of cards.

Mrs Felicia Hemans: Felicia Hemans (1796–1835) was an English poet, best known for 'The Homes of England' and 'Casabianca' (quoted by Irma in Chapter 3).

Spindle-shank: a person with long, thin legs.

Truckle bed: or 'trundle bed', a bed on castors that can be stored under a larger bed.

Q What effect do the first-person narratives have on the novel?

Q How is the combative relationship between Sara and Mrs Appleyard established?

Key point

The fact that Irma trails off when reciting 'Casabianca' suggests that she, like Sara, does not excel at memorising poetry, perhaps an early hint that Mrs Appleyard unfairly targets Sara, or perhaps a critique of learning by rote. The novel also seems to suggest that Felicia Hemans wrote 'The Wreck of the Hesperus'; she did not, but 'Casabianca' is also about the destruction of a ship, and was a staple of school readers for a century.

Chapter 5 (pp.58–78)

Summary: *The college tries to keep the news of the girls' disappearance secret; the search continues and the police interview witnesses; Mrs Appleyard writes to the families.*

The girls and teachers respond in various ways to the shock of the previous day, from Mademoiselle's migraine to Edith's apparent amnesia – she remembers nothing of what frightened her at the Rock. Later in the chapter, Edith does recall both Greta McCraw approaching the Rock clad only in her underwear and a cloud of 'a nasty red colour' (p.73); the latter is one of the moments in the book that readers often cite as evidence of supernatural (or, in some readings, extraterrestrial) intervention in the girls' disappearance.

Despite the attempt to keep the news secret, this chapter focuses on gossip – from the 'official' gossip of Edith's report to the police about Miss McCraw to the unofficial gossip spreading through the town and, via newspapers, more broadly. The outward spread of gossip is one of Lindsay's uses of a 'rippling' pattern in the novel.

The focus on police procedure in this chapter might mislead the reader into thinking the novel will be a traditional whodunnit, which is not borne out by the rest of the narrative.

Key vocabulary

Black tracker: an Indigenous expert in surveillance and tracking, sometimes formally employed by the police force (for example, the Queensland Native Mounted Police Force) and sometimes employed as needed.

Les pantalons / drawers: knee-length undergarments worn under a petticoat.

Strawberry cob: a cob is a small, stout and generally placid horse. 'Strawberry' refers to a reddish coat.

Q How does Lindsay's description of the landscape relate to the problematic concept of *terra nullius*?

Q Apart from the red cloud, is there any other indication of supernatural intervention in the disappearances?

Key point

Ngannelong (Hanging Rock) is significant to the Dja Dja Wurrung, Woi Wurrung and Taungurung people, who were forcibly displaced after the colonists' arrival in the area in the mid-nineteenth century. Although Lindsay creates a complex interplay between colonial domestic spaces and the Australian landscape in the novel, Aboriginal people and perspectives are relatively absent, with the exception of the unnamed and voiceless black tracker who is first mentioned on page 62. Some Aboriginal writers have responded to Lindsay's story: Gomeroi poet Alison Whittaker's 'Many Girls White Linen' (2017) is one such reflection on the original and ongoing Aboriginal custodianship of the site and the violence of colonial usurpation.

Chapter 6 (pp.79–89)

Summary: *Michael convinces Albert to help him search the Rock.*

This is the first chapter showing Albert and Michael in the state of friendship that began at the Rock on the day of the picnic, when Michael told Albert to call him 'Mike'. Just as Mrs Appleyard and Sara's is the strongest negative relationship in the novel, Michael and Albert's friendship is the strongest positive relationship. The two relationships are set in contrast even more powerfully when the reader realises that Sara and Albert are siblings.

In this chapter, Michael is beginning to pull away from the liminal state in which we met him ('A slender fair youth – or a very young man', p.30), and becoming more independent. This is marked by his rejection of his aunt's garden party (representing the milieu in which he was raised) in favour of having an Australian beer with Albert (reflecting the egalitarianism of his chosen home), and continues through his refusal to meet people's expectations that he will marry Irma.

Key vocabulary

New chum: a slang term for a newly arrived immigrant, implying the person is inexperienced and naive.

Rouse-about: an unskilled labourer or odd-job worker, particular during shearing season. A rouse-about was usually itinerant, moving from farm to farm.

Russell Street blokes: the headquarters of the Melbourne police were at Russell Street from the 1850s, although the well-known Russell Street Police Headquarters was only built in the 1940s.

Q To what extent might Michael be changing before the girls go missing? Or is his change driven entirely by the disappearances?

Chapter 7 (pp.90–104)

Summary: *Albert and Michael search Hanging Rock; Albert leaves at sundown, but Michael remains overnight.*

Michael's obsession with Miranda – the only one of the girls he thinks of by name, rather than by description, such as 'the little dark one' (Irma) or 'the dumpy fat one' (Edith) – becomes clearer in this chapter, as he hallucinates her laughing in the bush around him. It is not the last time he has a hallucination of Miranda: he later sees her standing on his father's lawn, and the regular references to swans also evoke his obsession.

Michael's search for the girls on Hanging Rock brings him, seemingly, into the same sphere of the uncanny as the girls: like them (but perhaps unlike Greta McCraw), he is generally fine at the Picnic Grounds, but becomes more and more disorientated the higher he climbs. None of the other searchers seem to report similar effects, so why this is the case for Michael is a mystery.

Key vocabulary

Agincourt: a battle fought on 25 October 1415, during the Hundred Years' War, in which the English beat the French; 'Agincourt' is often used as a patriotic rallying cry.

Boer War: the Second Boer War (1899–1902) between the British Empire and two Boer states (independent Dutch-speaking colonies) in South Africa, supported by soldiers from Australia, which was then still a British colony.

Collins Street doctors: doctors with Melbourne practices who have country homes in the area. The top end of Collins Street was dominated by medical practices at this time.

'On your Pat Malone': rhyming slang for 'alone'. Said to originate in the ballad 'Paddy Malone in Australia', in which the central character is an Irish immigrant.

Sugar-doodle: to slip or fall over.

Q Does Lindsay give any indication of why only some people are affected by the Rock?

Q What differences do we see between how the Rock affects the girls and how it affects Michael?

Chapter 8 (pp.105–26)

Summary: *Albert returns to Hanging Rock, finding Michael injured and Irma unconscious but unharmed.*

When found, Irma bears strange injuries: her bare feet are perfectly clean and uninjured, although the bodice of her dress is bloody (p.119), as is her hair (p.120), and her hands are bruised and the nails badly torn (p.121). Her petticoat, drawers and camisole (all underwear) are torn and dusty (p.121), and although she is otherwise fully dressed, except for her stockings and shoes, she is no longer wearing the corset she had on when she disappeared (p.121). The injuries are explained in the missing chapter of the novel, but are perhaps more effective left unexplained.

The novel emphasises that she has not been raped (p.121), which has clearly been the suggestion behind the questions posed to Albert and Michael earlier. Mrs Appleyard later openly muses on this as a reason for the disappearances (p.225), and the Melbourne police also suggest it (p.131).

Key vocabulary

Flamdoodle: nonsense.

Open-work stockings: stockings with decorative gaps in the fabric, giving a lacy effect.

Q Why might Irma's injuries be described in such detail, even though we don't find out their cause?

Chapter 9 (pp.127–41)

Summary: *Irma's rescue is announced at the college; search parties continue to look for the other girls.*

Mrs Appleyard struggles to influence the mood of the college, firstly through a relaxation of daily rituals (trips to the theatre, evening entertainments) and then through a tightening of restrictions (enforcing the rule of silence among the girls). Despite her attempts, parents begin withdrawing their girls from the college, including Irma Leopold's father.

This is the beginning stage of a widening sphere of influence, as the consequences of the disappearances spread to involve a larger and larger group of people, through gossip, destruction of plans, financial consequences and more. Up to this chapter, the novel has focused on the effects on the close circle at Appleyard College. Lindsay's editor recalled that 'she was fascinated by patterns, by things rippling out from a centre and influencing other things' (McCulloch 2017, p.151), and this preoccupation is evident in this chapter.

Key vocabulary

Black Forest: a wooded area in the Mount Macedon region, which was a haunt of bushrangers in the gold rush period.

Olympus: the home of the gods in Greek mythology.

Racine: Jean Racine (1639–99), a popular and influential tragic playwright of seventeenth-century France.

Rothschild: a famous German banking family. The children of Mayer Amschel Rothschild (1744–1812) set up banking dynasties in England, France, Austria and Naples, making them one of the wealthiest families in modern history.

Q 'A "situation" cannot be pigeonholed for reference and the appropriate answer pulled out of a filing cabinet' (p.129). To what extent does this sentence summarise the mood of the novel?

Chapter 10 (pp.142–57)

Summary: *Irma and Michael recuperate together across the remaining weeks of summer.*

Lindsay continues the theme of the mystery's widening sphere of influence. An event that at first affected only the four girls and their mistress, and then their schoolmates and families, spreads out to affect more and more people, as news of the disappearances travels on 'the Macedon grapevine' (p.144).

Irma's love for Michael is another element of the novel that defies the linear passage of time: her reflection that she knew he was her beloved from her first sight of him (p.167) makes the relationship seem fixed to a specific moment in time, as does the narrator casting forward to explain that Michael's image 'would come to her in the Bois de Boulogne, under the trees in Hyde Park' (p.157). Albert's experience of a conversation with Irma expanding 'to fill the entire content of a summer afternoon' (p.154) suggests the same phenomenon.

Key vocabulary

Halma: a strategy board game invented by American George Howard Monks around 1883. Chinese checkers is a later variant of Halma, using a star-shaped rather than square board.

Marrons glacés: candied chestnuts soaked in sugar syrup and then glazed.

Snakes and Ladders: an ancient Indian board game, marketed under the name Snakes and Ladders in England.

'Two Little Girls in Blue': a music-hall song from 1893, written by Charles Graham. In it, an old man regrets his unwarranted jealousy, which caused his wife to leave him.

Q To what extent does Lindsay create romantic love as something both immediate and permanent?

Q Why is Irma unable to sway Michael from his obsession with Miranda?

Chapter 11 (pp.158–67)

Summary: *Michael announces his departure from Lake View; Irma reflects on her love for him.*

Chapters 10 and 11 together contain the extent of Irma and Michael's part-friendship, part-courtship. This chapter, in particular, reinforces the extent to which Irma belongs to the world that Michael is trying to shake off: she is effortlessly charming and comfortable in Mrs Fitzhubert's drawing room at Lake View, even with the disappointment of Michael's absence.

The storm that breaks when Irma is about to read Michael's letter recalls the poetic device of the 'pathetic fallacy', in which nature reflects the mood of the poet. Irma, outwardly cool and calm, is inwardly storming; even before she reads the letter, she is aware (as the storm indicates) that it marks a cooling-off of their friendship.

Key vocabulary

Aubusson: hand-woven carpets made in central France. While Axminster (Chapter 1) are high-quality machine-made carpets, Aubusson are of significantly higher quality, reflecting Irma's wealth.

Backboard: a rigid board to which a person can be strapped, usually used to improve the posture of young girls.

Leghorn hat: a finely plaited straw hat with a wide brim.

'Plump little Empress of India': Queen Victoria, who became Empress of India in 1876. Balmoral Castle in Aberdeenshire, Scotland, was a favoured residence of Victoria.

Q Are there other examples in the text where nature reflects the mood of the characters?

Q Why does Michael break off his relationship with Irma?

Chapter 12 (pp.168–83)

Summary: *Irma visits the college on her way to Melbourne; Mrs Appleyard receives a letter from Mr Leopold threatening a full investigation; the girls demand Irma reveal the truth.*

The key scene in this chapter is the mobbing of Irma by the other students. The mass hysteria recalls historical moments of shared hallucinations or delusions, including the dancing plague of 1518 (Strasbourg, Alsace), the Salem witch trials (Massachusetts, United States, 1692–93) and an outbreak of screaming and trance at a convent in Würzburg, Germany, in 1749. Mademoiselle, when she describes it later in her life, even draws on imagery of the French Revolution (1789–99), which had moments of group hysteria.

In Chapter 9, with the announcement of Irma's return, Lindsay notes, 'An atmosphere can be generated overnight out of nothing or everything, anywhere that human beings are congregated in unnatural conditions' (p.129), foreshadowing this hysteria.

Irma is also the first of the significant departures of the novel: after her, Minnie and Tom, Dora and Mademoiselle all leave the college, as do various students.

Key vocabulary

Bloomers: long, loose shorts, usually tied below the knee, designed to be worn during exercise.

Indian club: bowling-pin-shaped wooden clubs used in strength and mobility training.

Malheureusement: a French word meaning regrettably or unfortunately.

'Men of Harlech': a military march, the music of which was first published in 1794.

Normandy hares: Hares are hunted in Normandy, France, on strictly controlled dates.

Q What is the effect of the scenes of hysteria in the novel?

Key point

The term hysteria derives from the Greek word for uterus and was considered to be a female ailment, so setting the main scene of hysteria in the college gymnasium is suggestive. It reinforces the division between the artificial 'lady', dressed in gloves and complete with socially mandated deportment, and a natural 'woman', who has a body that can display strength and emotion. In the description of the gymnasium as 'the Chamber of Horrors' (p.173) and a space that 'proclaimed Authority's high-handed disregard of Nature's basic laws' (p.174), Lindsay offers an encapsulation of the theme of society versus nature. See 'Themes, ideas & values' for a further discussion.

Chapter 13 (pp.184–96)

Summary: *Dora Lumley's brother arrives to announce her resignation; Sara becomes ill; Dora and her brother are killed in a hotel fire.*

Although the key event in this chapter is the departure and death of Dora Lumley, it also contains a number of small, significant moments that contribute to Mrs Appleyard's increasing lack of control:

- the departure of various students at their parents' behest (pp.186–7)
- the note from Melbourne police saying they wanted to look into 'one or two points concerning matters of school discipline prior to the day of the Picnic' (p.187)
- the letters from Mr Leopold and Miranda's father that Mrs Appleyard avoids answering (p.185)
- the rumours that are beginning to spread about the college being 'haunted' (p.186).

With these factors combined, Mrs Appleyard loses control not only with Reg Lumley, but also with Sara. We do not see her interview with Sara, but it must be the occasion on which Sara cries 'Not that! Not the orphanage!' (p.227) – an exclamation that later haunts Mrs Appleyard, since Sara dies sometime between this chapter and the next.

Q How is Dora's death a consequence of the events at Hanging Rock?

Q Although she is a minor character, what is the significance of Dora's role in the novel?

Chapter 14 (pp.197–212)

Summary: *Michael returns briefly from Melbourne to his uncle's home; Albert receives a cheque for his role in rescuing Irma.*

This chapter concludes three parts of the 'pattern begun at Hanging Rock' (p.197).

- Michael makes up his mind to go to Queensland, to Miranda's family station, Goonawingi. The departure of the swans (p.199), which Michael has always associated with Miranda, might suggest that his obsession with her is over, but his plans to visit her family station suggest otherwise (p.201).
- Albert is given the opportunity, and then the means, to accompany Michael, with the cheque for £1000 from Irma's father.
- Tom and Minnie, the faithful school servants, pursue work that suits and appeals to them both, with Tom taking Albert's place at Lake View.

Although the reader is not aware of it at this stage, the chapter also includes the end of a fourth pattern, as Albert recounts his dream of his sister, bidding her farewell.

Key vocabulary

Bobby-dazzler: anything outstanding or striking.

Boule table: an extravagantly inlaid and gold-embossed piece of French furniture, named after maker André-Charles Boulle.

Castlemaine Wonder: while no boxer by this name has been identified, 'Wonder' (usually combined with a birthplace) is a common boxing nickname.

Norman tower: the Norman dynasty in England began in 1066 with William the Conqueror and ended in 1154 under King Stephen. The tower emphasises the ancientness of Michael's family.

Strapper: someone who looks after racehorses.

Q For some characters, the disappearance of the girls leads to personal opportunities, while for others, the opposite is true. What might Lindsay be telling the reader through the characters' fates?

Chapter 15 (pp.213–31)

Summary: *Mademoiselle becomes concerned when Mrs Appleyard announces that Sara has left with her guardian; Mrs Appleyard searches Sara's room late at night.*

The specifics of Sara's fate remain something of a mystery: has she committed suicide?

The strongest implication is that she has, out of fear of being returned to the orphanage – for example, Mrs Appleyard finds and removes a note pinned to Sara's pincushion (p.227). However, it is unclear whether Mrs Appleyard knows that Sara has committed suicide or whether she believes she has run away; if she does know that Sara is dead, presumably she believes the girl has killed herself somewhere away from the college, given her shock at the body in the hydrangeas. Either way, Mrs Appleyard makes a conscious attempt to deceive her staff, removing some of Sara's personal items in a covered basket and informing Mademoiselle that Sara's guardian had called for her. The 2018 television adaptation took advantage of this uncertainty to depict Mrs Appleyard as Sara's murderer.

Key vocabulary

Christmas lilies: also known as amaryllis; a long-lasting, trumpet-shaped flower.

Indian summer: a period of unusually warm, dry weather, usually in autumn. 'Indian summer' is an American term; the phenomenon has also been called 'second summer'.

Loquacious: talkative.

Trousseaux: (plural of trousseau) the possessions, especially clothes and household linens, gathered by a bride for her marriage.

Q What do the varying fates of Albert and Sara tell us about the way in which social class is treated in the novel?

Q Why does Mrs Appleyard lie about Sara leaving with her guardian?

Key point

The depiction of Appleyard College in this chapter is sinister, particularly the moment where Mrs Appleyard pauses on the landing and hears the clock ticking like a heartbeat (p.226). What had been a benign space early in the novel has become dishevelled and perhaps malignant. Suzette Mayr's essay (2017) is an excellent engagement with this uncanny aspect of the novel.

Chapter 16 (pp.232–44)

Summary: *Constable Bumpher receives a letter from Mademoiselle about Sara; Mr Whitehead, the gardener, finds Sara's body; Mrs Appleyard makes a final trip out to Hanging Rock.*

Mrs Appleyard's walk up the Rock recalls the imagery of Miranda and the others walking the same path. For example, like them, she removes some of the visible trappings of her class, such as her gloves, although she does not go so far as to remove her shoes and corset. However, whereas the girls are depicted as 'sliding over the stones on their bare feet as if they were on a drawing-room carpet' (p.44), Mrs Appleyard remains a 'heavy flat-footed woman' (p.243): she is drawn to their path, but she never occupies the bush in the uncanny fashion they do. Unlike them, her fate is explicitly, even grotesquely, detailed, as the reader is given an image of the body 'bouncing and rolling from rock to rock' and 'impaled upon a jutting crag' (p.244).

Q Why is Mrs Appleyard drawn to Hanging Rock?

Q Why does Lindsay leave some aspects of Sara's death ambiguous?

Chapter 17 (pp.245–6)

Summary: *A newspaper article summarises the events between Mrs Appleyard's death and 1913, thirteen years later.*

Embedding fictional newspaper articles in a novel is a common technique to lend an air of authenticity to a narrative. The newspaper article here forms a bookend with Lindsay's introductory author's note: 'Whether *Picnic at Hanging Rock* is fact or fiction, my readers must decide for themselves.' Together, they destablise the fictionality of the novel, invoking the idea that the story may be based on fact. The newspaper article also provides a sense of closure around some characters (Edith's death, Irma's marriage), which serves to reinforce the absence of an explanation for the overall mystery.

Key vocabulary

Marie Celeste: the *Mary Celeste* (often referred to as *Marie Celeste*) was a merchant ship found drifting and uninhabited in the Atlantic Ocean in 1872; what happened to her crew remains a great maritime mystery.

Society for Psychical Research: a real organisation, founded in England in 1882. It is the first body in the world established to study psychic phenomena.

Q What is Lindsay's purpose in suggesting that the novel might be a true story?

CHARACTERS & RELATIONSHIPS

Miranda

Key quotes

'Let me tell you this, Mrs Appleyard: anything of the slightest importance that I learned here at the College I learned from Miranda.' (Irma, p.172)

'What was her name, the tall pale girl with straight yellow hair, who had gone skimming over the water like one of the white swans on his Uncle's lake?' (p.34)

Miranda – tall, blonde and pale – is the eldest child and only daughter of a well-established squatter family, and head girl of Appleyard College. Unlike the other characters, Miranda is always and only addressed by her first name: even her parents are only identified as 'Miranda's father' and 'Miranda's mother'. The emphasis on her first name underscores Miranda's centrality to both the school and the story: we do not need a surname, because everyone knows who Miranda is. But it also gives Miranda a fairytale-like quality, and evokes comparisons with Shakespeare's Miranda in *The Tempest*, a child raised far from civilisation whose primary playmate is a spirit of the air. Miranda is an enigmatic figure in the novel, experienced through other characters' responses to her: while the third-person narration allows us to see inside some of the characters' minds (notably Irma Leopold and Michael Fitzhubert), we are not given a glimpse of Miranda's thought processes.

Miranda is fond of both her home and her family: she treasures her baby brother's valentine more than all the others she receives (p.8). Miranda also thinks longingly of the bush around her home, a Northern Queensland cattle station (p.9). Her upbringing has made her strong, competent and considerate: she opens the gate at Hanging Rock for the carriage without being asked, expertly manipulating the crooked timber (p.21), and helps the other girls ascend the Rock (p.39). Gentle, kind and charitable, she is also a leader among the girls: for example, Marion and

Irma look to her for permission when Edith asks to join the walk to the Rock (p.28).

Characters refer to Miranda in metaphors: Michael thinks of her as a swan (p.34, p.96, p.123, p.148); Mademoiselle as a Botticelli angel (p.28); and the gardener as a Christmas lily – which, in a cyclical return to Mademoiselle's vision, remind Miranda herself of angels (p.229).

Irma Leopold

Key quotes

'Radiantly lovely at seventeen, the little heiress was without personal vanity or pride of possession.' (p.9)

'Even as a little girl, Irma Leopold had wanted above all things to see everyone happy with the cake of their choice.' (p.38)

The daughter of extremely wealthy parents who live an extravagant lifestyle, Irma is a prized student for Mrs Appleyard not only because of the fees her father pays, but also because her presence will help attract the daughters of other wealthy men. Her significance is indicated by the fact that it is to her parents that Mrs Appleyard writes first (p.76). Like Sara, Irma is deeply fond of Miranda, telling Mrs Appleyard that 'anything of the slightest importance that I learned here at the College I learned from Miranda' (p.172). She is the only disappeared girl to return from the Rock.

Irma leaves Australia when Michael, still obsessed with the vanished Miranda, has put an end to any suggestion of romance between them; she returns to England with her parents. Irma remains kind and open-hearted even after the events of the novel, giving 'handsome donations to a thousand lost causes – lepers, sinking theatrical companies, missionaries, priests, tubercular prostitutes, saints, lame dogs and deadbeats all over the world' (p.38). The last reference to her in the novel indicates that she is now – thirteen years after the disappearances, when she would be thirty years old – the Countess de Latte-Marguery and living in Europe.

Mademoiselle Dianne de Poitiers

Key quotes

'The Headmistress knew a lady when she saw one, and Mademoiselle de Poitiers was definitely a social asset on the staff, not to be easily replaced.' (p.132)

'"Why is it, Miranda," she [Irma] whispered, "that such a sweet pretty creature is a school-teacher – of all dreary things in the world …?"' (p.26)

An elegant blonde woman only a few years older than the senior boarders, Mademoiselle de Poitiers teaches French conversation and dance at Appleyard College, and looks after the girls' attire (p.10). She is an 'endearing presence' (p.193) at the college, and a necessary counterbalance to the impersonality of Miss McGraw, the severity of Mrs Appleyard and the dreariness of Miss Lumley. As such, she is a strong influence on the girls, capable, for example, of disrupting the panic in the classroom when Miss Lumley hides to avoid facing it.

Raised 'among the great European galleries' (p.11), she interprets her environment through the traditions of Western art, imagining Irma 'against a background of cherries and pineapples, cherubs and golden flagons' (p.11), and seeing Miranda as 'a Botticelli angel from the Uffizi' (p.28). She is a religious woman, who draws increasing strength from her faith as the situation develops: after the moment of hysteria in the gymnasium, 'she was no longer afraid of Mrs Appleyard's individual wrath, now rendered impotent by the impersonal wrath of Heaven' (p.193).

Michael Fitzhubert

Key quotes

'… the English youth whose own ancient name was a valuable personal possession that travelled everywhere with him, like his pigskin valise and well-filled notecase …' (p.33)

'There was only one conscious thought in his head: Go on. A Fitzhubert ancestor hacking his way through bloody barricades at Agincourt had felt much the same way …' (p.104)

The Honourable Michael Fitzhubert is the grandson of the Earl of Haddingham (p.204) and the son of a Conservative member of the House of Lords (p.81), educated at an English public school and, briefly, at the University of Cambridge (p.165). Rather shy and inarticulate, he befriends his uncle's coachman, Albert Crundall, while staying with his aunt and uncle near Appleyard College. He is with Albert when they see the girls walking towards Hanging Rock, and it is Albert who finds him when he discovers the unconscious Irma.

Newly arrived in Australia – only three weeks before the picnic (p.65) – Michael is at a transitional point, somewhere between 'a slender fair youth – or a very young man' (p.30). He also transitions between the titles 'the Honourable Michael Fitzhubert' and 'Mike', the name he asks Albert to use 'unless my Aunt's listening' (p.33). Michael represents a potential that mirrors how Australia is represented in the novel: 'Australia, where anything might happen. In England, everything had been done before: quite often by one's own ancestors, over and over again' (p.34). As the novel continues, he matures into a man who rejects his English past for an Australian future.

Michael demonstrates an ongoing fascination with Miranda, from the moment he sees her crossing the creek at Hanging Rock. He repeatedly thinks of her as a swan (p.34, p.96, p.123, p.148), including in a sequence where he imagines her standing over the birdbath on his uncle's lawn, only to see a swan take flight (p.148). The obsession becomes the key influence on his life, and he eventually leaves the region; we find in the final chapter that he is still living and working on 'a station property in Northern Queensland' (p.246), presumably Miranda's family property of Goonawingi, which he mentions to Albert earlier (p.201).

Albert Crundall

Key quotes

'It was a new sensation for Albert to be troubled by anything beyond his own immediate affairs and he didn't care for it.' (p.105)

'Some of Albert's more hair-raising anecdotes were true, others not. It made no odds.' (p.81)

Albert is an orphan – he was brought up in a Ballarat orphanage with his sister, Sara (p.30). He is the son of an itinerant farm worker (a rouse-about) who 'used to change his name now and then when he got in a tight corner' (p.33) and a woman who 'cleared out with a bloke from Sydney' (p.32). He bears tattoos of mermaids on his arms, which he tells Michael a sailor did for him in Sydney when he was fifteen (p.80). He and Michael are both twenty when the novel opens (p.81). He is skilled with horses, and has the respect of Colonel Fitzhubert, for whom he works as coachman.

Along with Michael, he is one of the last people to see the girls before they disappear, bringing him under suspicion. A working-class man, he gently mocks Michael's full name – the Honourable Michael Fitzhubert – claiming that he wouldn't recognise his own name 'if I was to see it written down in print' (p.33). The one example of his writing – a letter to Irma's father (pp.210–11) – demonstrates that Albert is literate, but not comfortably so: Lindsay describes him as 'almost illiterate' (p.81). Although he is valued by his employer, the cheque from Irma's father gives him an unprecedented opportunity to pursue his own ambitions, and he follows Michael to Queensland. Albert's fate is not mentioned in the final chapter.

Mrs Appleyard

Key quotes

'Born fifty-seven years ago in a suburban wilderness of smoke-grimed bricks, she knew no more of Nature than a scarecrow rigid on a broomstick above a field of waving corn.' (p.243)

'Now an immense purposeful figure was swimming and billowing in grey silk taffeta on the tiled and colonnaded verandah, like a galleon in full sail.' (p.13)

Fifty-seven years old, Mrs Appleyard is an English-born widow who arrived in Australia and established Appleyard College six years before the events of the novel. Little is revealed of her husband, Arthur, except that she thinks of him fondly, dreams of him often (p.45) and draws on memories of his support: she imagines him saying that her letters to the families are 'masterly' (p.77), for example, and remembers 'complacently' that 'he had always … called her his financial genius' (p.46).

Like her college, she is a bastion of Victorian sensibility: described throughout the novel as magisterial, dressed in rich silk taffeta, with her hair elaborately arranged, wearing a cameo portrait of her late husband (p.13). The consequences of the mystery at Hanging Rock can be seen clearly in the difference between Mrs Appleyard's first appearance, on the balcony (p.13), and one of her last, creeping through the house at midnight, an 'old woman with head bowed under a forest of curling pins, with pendulous breasts and sagging stomach beneath a flannel dressing-gown' (p.226).

Mrs Appleyard's reasons for coming to Australia are not explained in the book. Although she has a 'considerable nest-egg' (p.7), she also worries about the loss of income when students are withdrawn from the college (p.186); possibly, she is seeking greater financial opportunities. There is also a suggestion that she has not always been financially independent: contemplating the damage to the college's reputation, the narrator reflects that 'in the past Mrs Appleyard and her Arthur had skated hand in hand over some remarkably thin ice' (p.186). This might also explain her fear of losing the security (both social and financial) offered by the college.

One marker of Mrs Appleyard's decline is the increasing frequency with which she drinks brandy. Before she is aware that the girls have disappeared, 'there was still enough left in the decanter since the Bishop of Bendigo had lunched at the College' (p.48), but by the time Irma departs, Mrs Appleyard's hand 'seized with an uncontrollable tremor, reached for the bottle of cognac under the desk' (p.172).

Sara Waybourne

Key quotes

'Those great saucer eyes, holding a perpetual unspoken criticism intolerable in a child of thirteen.' (p.76)

'The small pointed face was somehow the symbol of the nameless malady from which every inmate of the College was suffering in varying degrees.' (p.134)

An orphan whose school fees are paid by an elderly guardian, Sara Waybourne is one of the youngest students at Appleyard College, a small, thin girl who rooms with and adores Miranda. Raised in an orphanage, her key childhood memory is telling people that she 'thought it would be fun to be a lady circus rider on a lovely white horse in a spangled dress' (p.195) and having her head shaved so she could not run away. She is described as thirteen years old, but tells the maid, Minnie, that 'I don't know. Even my guardian doesn't know for certain' (p.195).

Although it is never stated outright, Sara is Albert Crundall's younger sister: she calls for 'Bertie' in her distress (p.47); Albert says that 'some old geezer took a fancy to her a few years ago' (p.93); Albert's sister's favourite flowers, pansies (p.93), are also Sara's favourite (p.229); and Albert's elaborate dream of his sister coming to say goodbye to him (pp.202–3) occurs on the night of Sara's death. In this sense, Sara's death repeats the pattern of disappearances in the novel: Albert (presumably) never knows what happens to his sister, just as we never learn what happens to the missing girls.

Mrs Appleyard recognises in Sara a will of steel resembling her own (p.134), which makes her resent the youngest pupil, a sentiment that is exacerbated by her guardian's failure to pay the term's fees. The novel implies that Mrs Appleyard is severe towards Sara before the disappearances: Sara is prevented from attending the picnic because of a failure to memorise a poem (p.12), but Irma's comment 'I forget the rest of it' (p.41) indicates that she too is poor at memorisation. However, after the disappearances, Mrs Appleyard sees Sara as representative of the troubles affecting the college, and increases her mistreatment. This cruel behaviour is mimicked by junior mistress Dora Lumley – for example, when she leaves Sara strapped to the backboard (p.183). The only mistresses to show kindness to Sara are Mademoiselle de Poitiers and art teacher Mrs Valange.

Edith Horton

Key quotes

'Such abandoned folly would always be beyond the understanding of Edith and her kind, who early in life take to woollen bedsocks and galoshes.' (p.42)

'In the novel role of ringleader Edith was beside herself, smugly wagging a stumpy forefinger.' (p.178)

Edith Horton is one of the younger students in the college: a 'pasty-faced fourteen-year-old with the contours of an overstuffed bolster' (p.12), she is regularly called 'fat' or 'dumpy' (p.28) and demonstrates a degree of greed. Not a particularly engaging character, and a 'somewhat shadowy figure' (p.246) – as the newspaper article at the novel's end calls her – she is significant in the text as the only one who returns from the Rock, becoming a foil for Miranda's effect on the novel.

Edith is not an intelligent child. This may be in part the result of her upbringing: she mentions at one point that her mother believes a woman's place is in the home and does not want Edith learning abstruse subjects such as mathematics (p.73). With Miranda and Marion gone, she is in a position of greater power among the girls and is the ringleader of the group that surrounds Irma in the gymnasium (p.178), even though she herself is stricken with terror by the situation (p.176).

Edith dies in Melbourne somewhere around 1913 (p.247), in her late twenties. She remains a figure of interest in the mystery, and the newspaper article hints that she might have clung to the mystery as something that gave her intrigue and notoriety.

Marion Quade

Key quote

> 'There was no real rancour in Marion – only a burning desire for truth in all departments.' (p.38)

The daughter of a Queen's Counsel (deceased), Marion Quade is a close friend of Miranda and Irma, with a thin face and legs and a 'sensitive nose that appeared to be always on the scent of something long awaited and sought' (p.10). Not as wealthy as Irma and Miranda, she 'could be counted on for academic laurels, almost equally important in their way' (p.76). Marion calls her guardian a 'dodderer' (p.78), and he seems uninvolved in her life, other than covering the expenses of her education.

Although Lindsay suggests that there is no rancour in Marion, she demonstrates an inclination to tease less intelligent students in a manner that perhaps does not quite rise to the level of bullying: for example, when Edith starts to panic at the approach to Hanging Rock, Marion teases her despite Edith's distress, calling her a 'little goose' (p.37) and reflecting dispassionately, 'I always thought she was a stupid child and now I know' (p.38). However, when the students experience their moment of mass hysteria in the gymnasium, they think of Marion as well as Miranda (p.176), so she is not entirely unpopular among them.

Greta McCraw

Key quote

'Climate meant nothing, nor fashion, nor the never ending miles of gum trees and dry yellow grass, of which she was hardly more aware than of the mists and mountains of her native Scotland, as a girl.' (p.12)

Forty-five-year-old Greta McCraw, the mathematics mistress at Appleyard College, is 'far too brilliant for her poorly paid job' (p.11). She has been in Australia for nearly thirty years, but Mrs Appleyard notes that she 'has not a single friend, or acquaintance even, on this side of the world' (p.61). However, Mrs Appleyard values her 'cool appraisement' and, after her disappearance, regrets the loss of 'this woman of masculine intellect on whom she had come to rely in the last years' (p.225). Miss McCraw's is the most mysterious of the disappearances (she is not with the others, but has apparently been drawn to the Rock from as far as the Picnic Grounds), and perhaps the most melancholic: while everyone thinks fondly of Miranda – to the point of obsession, in more than one case – and the girls also think of Marion, only Mrs Appleyard seems to remember and regret Miss McCraw, and that belatedly.

Dora Lumley

Key quote

'I am a truthful woman, Mr Lumley, and if you don't know it already allow me to tell you that your sister is a bad-tempered, ignorant dunce'. (Mrs Appleyard, p.191)

Dora Lumley is a junior mistress at Appleyard College. She has a brother, Reginald (Reg) Lumley, of whom she is fond and whose character she admires, although the narrator refers to him as the 'drab unspeakable brother' (p.8) and Irma denigrates him as 'dreary' (p.9). She is not involved at the events at Hanging Rock, but is affected by their consequences, ultimately losing her job and almost immediately dying in a hotel fire.

THEMES, IDEAS & VALUES

Nature versus society

Key quotes

'Appleyard College was already, in the year nineteen hundred, an architectural anachronism in the Australian bush – a hopeless misfit in time and place.' (p.6)

'Swathes of virgin forest ran right down to an immaculate tennis lawn, an orchard, a row of raspberry canes.' (p.92)

Throughout the novel, Lindsay explores the tension between the natural environment and the built environment, especially (but not exclusively) Appleyard College. The college is introduced to the reader before any of the actual characters, first through its furnishings – mantelpieces of 'white marble' and 'carved and tortured wood embellished with a thousand winking tiddling mirrors' (p.6) – and then, as though we pan outwards, the exterior, a 'clumsy two storey mansion' that 'was one of those elaborate houses that sprang up all over Australia like exotic fungi following the finding of gold' (p.6). Appleyard College, then, is temporally and chronologically specific: a mid-Victorian house settled midway between Melbourne and the goldfields that were the site of great activity in the gold rush of the 1850s. The house sits uncomfortably in its environment, with an 'insignificant creek' and 'occasional glimpses' of nearby Mount Macedon through 'a screen of stringy-barked eucalyptus' (p.6). This prefigures the way in which the girls in their elaborate Edwardian outfits at Hanging Rock Picnic Grounds 'were no more part of their environment than figures in a photograph album, arbitrarily posed against a backcloth of cork rocks and cardboard trees' (p.25).

The Picnic Grounds at Hanging Rock represent something of a midway point between nature and the built environment. They cannot be truly civilised: as long as the ancient rock hangs over them, they will always have something wild about them. The attempts to civilise them are somewhat half-hearted: 'manmade improvements on Nature at the Picnic Grounds consisted of several circles of flat stones to serve as fireplaces and a wooden privy in the shape of a Japanese pagoda' (p.23). But unlike the Rock itself, they retain the traces of human occupation: Albert and Michael notice when they return on their rescue mission that 'the ashes of their picnic fire still filled the blackened ring of the fireplace' (p.95). This is a safe-enough space for well-brought-up young ladies to picnic, provided it is remembered that 'the Rock itself is extremely dangerous' and that 'the vicinity is renowned for its venomous snakes and poisonous ants' (p.13). The Picnic Grounds are not nature tamed, but nature brought under some degree of control, unlike the Rock itself.

A more successful model of Edwardian society's ability to tame nature is in the houses that surround Colonel Fitzhubert's home of Lake View, at Mount Macedon. As Michael and Albert ride towards the Rock on their search-and-rescue mission, the 'road wound its charming leisurely way between sleeping gardens still heavy with dew and shadowed by the upper mountain slopes' (p.92). Like Appleyard College, the houses have been built in an alien landscape, but unlike the college, they occupy it more fittingly: where the college is clumsy and stands out from, rather than blends into, its environment, the houses of this wealthy community are positioned in a setting that has been carefully constructed: 'the undistinguished architecture of red roofed houses set among willow and maple, oak and elm' (p.92). Here is not nature tamed, precisely, but nature colonised, the stringy-barked eucalypts of Appleyard College replaced with lush European imports. Michael, a character amid a transition – no longer English but not yet entirely Australian – sees this place as also transitional, a 'strangely favoured country where palms, delphiniums and raspberry canes grew side by side' (p.93). Nor is Lindsay unsympathetic to this perspective: two of the kinder and more intuitive characters in the novel are the gardeners Edward Whitehead (Appleyard College) and Mr Cutler (Lake View). Albert, more practical, sees the expense involved in maintaining this illusion of British life, commenting that it 'costs a packet to live up here amongst the nobs' (p.93). Nature can be manipulated, planted, partially tamed, but not easily, and not cheaply.

A secondary aspect of the novel's concern with society versus nature is the tension between the artificial model of womanhood that is fostered through institutions such as Appleyard College and the 'natural girl' that is common in Australian literature. Australian fiction of the nineteenth century often presented Australian girls as hardier than their European counterparts, better at sport and horseriding, generally more attuned to the outdoors. Appleyard College – with its English headmistress, Scottish mathematics mistress and French dance mistress – is European society distilled: the poetry and the history that the girls are taught is European, rather than Australian. So too the socially accepted attire of the well-bred young woman, such as gloves and hats. The gardens in this school for the daughters of wealthy men distils the idea that British is better: the virgin forest of Australia is pruned and planted with English flowers, and could be seen as a metaphor for the education of these young Australian girls themselves.

Miranda is the only character to straddle the divide between the educated woman and the 'natural girl' effectively: her father recalls that she 'threw a leg over a horse like a boundary rider' at age five, while her mother says that she 'entered my drawing room with her head thrown back, like a little queen' (p.39). She is able to sublimate her longing for the bush – 'forests … with ferns and birds … like we have at home' (p.9) – and become a model schoolgirl. Some critics see Miranda as a figurative gatekeeper between nature and society – and she literally opens the gate to the Picnic Grounds allowing the carriage to pass 'out of the known dependable present and into the unknown future' (p.22). Perhaps this liminal state is what makes her vulnerable to the mysteries of the Rock.

The natural world

Key quotes

'"Except for those people over there in the wagonette we might be the only living creatures in the whole world," said Edith, airily dismissing the entire animal kingdom at one stroke.' (p.24)

'Confronted by such monumental configurations of nature the human eye is woefully inadequate.' (p.36)

Alongside the theme of attempts to tame or colonise nature, *Picnic at Hanging Rock* presents nature as far richer and more complex than its human occupants can ever realise. Nowhere is this more succinctly expressed than in the depiction of the picnic at the start of Chapter 2. As the girls eat 'chicken pie, angel cake, jellies' (p.23), Lindsay focuses the reader's attention on the activity of the natural world around them. In some instances, this activity is triggered by the picnic, as with the sugar ants 'laboriously dragging a piece of icing off the cake towards some subterranean larder' (p.24). In others, the two worlds are a reflection of each other: the 'diligent ants' with their 'never ending task of collecting and storing food' (p.24) are mirrored by Rosamund's 'fancywork' and the 'industrious sisters from New Zealand making pencil sketches' (p.25); the snakes that 'lay coiled in their secret holes awaiting the twilight hour' (p.25) recall the sleeping girls 'drugged with rich food and sunshine' (p.25); even Edith 'bumbling along' (p.28) on the way to the Rock recalls the 'clumsy armour-plated beetle' (p.25). And yet, after this elaborate mirroring of girls and nature, Lindsay is emphatic: 'the drowsy well-fed girls lounging in the shade were no more a part of their environment than figures in a photograph album' (p.25).

Moreover, despite this almost idyllic image of cohabitation, Lindsay shows that the human impact on the environment is inherently destructive. As Michael moves up the Rock, he is 'listening to the murmuring life of the forest welling up out of the warm green depth' (p.97). It seems initially an image of a man at peace and at one with nature. But his passage is injurious: 'Fronds of curled brown velvet snapped under his touch, his boots trod down the neat abodes of ants and spiders: his hand brushing against a streamer of bark dislodged a writhing colony of caterpillars' (p.97). Despite his sensitivity to the environment, in it he is a 'clumping monster' (p.97), 'with every step cutting a swathe of death and destruction through the dusty green' (p.98). The 'dusty green' recalls the image of Miranda approaching the Rock: 'They could see her straight yellow hair swinging loose above her thrusting shoulders, cleaving wave after wave of dusty green' (p.42). But, unlike Michael, Miranda and her disappearing fellows occupy the landscape more gently, even blending with it: while 'a sleeping lizard awoke and darted to safety' (p.97) from Michael, 'a horned lizard emerged from a crack to lie without fear in the hollow of Marion's outflung arm' (p.43); while Michael leaves the caterpillars 'brutally exposed to midday light' (p.97), Miranda wakes to a 'procession of queer looking beetles in bronze armour' making a 'leisurely crossing' of her ankle (p.43). Michael can come close to the girls' experience on the Rock, close enough to hear Miranda's laughter (p.103), but he cannot blend into the landscape as they do; he cannot disappear.

Lindsay reinforces this theme of destructiveness in the climactic image of the novel, the death of Mrs Appleyard. As with Michael, there are echoes of the girls' climb of the Rock in the description of Mrs Appleyard's climb, but negative imagery drives home the difference between the two expeditions – just as Edith sees the girls 'sliding over the stones on their bare feet as if they were on a drawing-room carpet' (p.44), Mrs Appleyard clambers over 'stones that slid from under her feet with every step' (p.244). Like Michael, she is a destructive force in the landscape, but where he destroys unthinkingly, with a brush of his hand, she destroys actively, seeking a stone with which to strike a spider 'spread-eagled, asleep in the sun' (p.244). So it is fitting that, despite Sara Waybourne's seemingly supernatural intervention (perhaps a genuine moment of the supernatural, perhaps the hallucination of a guilty mind), it is the Rock that strikes her down, in the visceral closing image of 'the head in the brown hat ... impaled upon a jutting crag' (p.244).

One curious feature of the Rock is its seemingly preternatural ability to wipe the trace of human activity. As early as Ben Hussey's statement to the police, we are told that Edith's footsteps 'had petered out almost at once on the stony ground' and that 'without a magnifying glass it was impossible to see anything in the way of a footprint' (p.55). Later, the bloodhound stood 'for nearly ten minutes growling and bristling at an almost circular platform of flat rock considerably further towards the summit' (p.87). We, the readers, have seen the girls, some forty pages earlier, standing on a 'semi-circular shelf' from which 'the plain below was just visible; infinitely vague and distant' (p.42), but here, even with the bloodhound's signal, 'the magnifying glass disclosed absolutely no signs of any disturbance more recent than the ravages of Nature over some hundreds or thousands of years' (p.87). Even Greta McCraw's clothes have entirely vanished, barring a 'small piece of frilled calico' (p.246) found years later.

Key point

Although Lindsay emphasises the vast age of Hanging Rock and its environs, she does not make any mention of the traditional owners of the area, nor of their expulsion in the 1830s by white settlers. And although the local police bring in an Indigenous tracker, we do not see him having any success in locating a trail (less success than the bloodhound): Lindsay seems to be suggesting that the Rock resists any and all human intervention, but one consequence of this, intentional or not, is the erasure of the relationship that the land's traditional owners have to the Rock. Note that the doctrine of *terra nullius* was not overturned in Australian law until 1992, and was still in force when Lindsay was writing.

Time

Key quotes

'The woman with the night-light stood listening to the tick-tock, tick-tock, coming up out of the shadows below.' (p.226)

'There is no single instant on this spinning globe that is not, for millions of individuals, immeasurable by ordinary standards of time: a fragment of eternity forever unrelated to the calendar or the striking clock.' (p.154)

Lindsay signposts clearly the period in which the events of *Picnic at Hanging Rock* take place. Readers can easily trace the six weeks over which the story occurs, through reference to specific dates: the picnic is on the auspicious date of 14 February, Valentine's Day; Mrs Appleyard's death is on 26 March; various dates are given in documents, providing a sense of the linear movement of time through the narrative. But at the same time, Lindsay disrupts this sense of time. Perhaps the most subtle example of this is the judicious repetition of imagery in the novel at the beginning and the end, from the hydrangeas (p.5, p.237) to the Axminster carpets (p.7, p.243). These repeated images suggest that time is in fact cyclical – much like in the students' history lessons, where 'the class were forever turning back for recapitulation at the death of King George the Fourth [1762–1830] before starting off again with Edward the Third [1312–1377] next term' (p.15).

More suggestive still are the moments when time slows, ceases or resists measurement. These begin as early as Chapter 1, which at first marks time and its passage strongly, with the information that the boarders have been awake since six a.m. (p.5) and Mademoiselle de Poitiers' repeated requests to 'hurry up' ('depêchez-vous', p.11). But once the girls and their mistresses leave the school, time begins to slow. Despite the steady movement of the horses and carriage, the world around stills: 'no traveller passed by, no bird song splintered the sunflecked silence, the grey pointed leaves of the saplings hung lifeless in the noonday heat' (p.19). Once they reach the Picnic Grounds at Hanging Rock, time behaves even more curiously, with watches and clocks either absent or inoperable, leaving the picknickers unable to tell the time except by 'looking knowingly at the shadow of the Hanging Rock which ever since luncheon had been creeping down towards the Picnic Grounds on the flat' (p.27).

The period between the departure of Miranda and the others and their disappearance is the period in which time is at its most fluid in the novel: from the moment Miranda smiles at Mademoiselle, to Mademoiselle's reflection that 'already the four girls must have been away for ten minutes, perhaps more' (p.29) is half a paragraph of text, an instant for the reader. The movement up the Rock, however, drags out in longer and longer periods, from the bright sunshine of the afternoon to the 'the colourless twilight' (p.43), which, in February, suggests the girls have been absent from the picnic for many hours. Nor can the girls' supernatural sleep explain the unaccounted-for hours. The sun is already going down when they see 'the face of a little cliff that held the last light of the sun' (p.42) before they fall asleep, and when they wake it is twilight. The text suggests that there is something about the Rock itself that warps either the movement or the measurement of time. Hours pass 'normally' at Appleyard College, but as the party approaches the Rock, time becomes increasingly fluid, and finally, on the slopes of the Rock itself, it lacks any resemblance to what we know as linear time. Some suggestion of this is present in the description of Mr Hussey driving his horses 'out of the known dependable present and into the unknown future' (p.22) when he travels through the gate into the Hanging Rock Picnic Grounds.

Time also appears as a motif in unexpected sections of the book: for example, Irma's memory, which is blank for the period of her disappearance, is described by the doctor as 'a clock that stops under a certain set of unusual conditions and refuses ever to go again beyond a particular point' (p.143). It is Miranda who offers one of the most striking symbols of the oppressive nature of the artificial measurement of time. Asked about her 'pretty little diamond watch', she tells Mademoiselle she no longer wears it: 'I can't stand hearing it ticking all day long just above my heart' (p.27). The novel privileges a natural measurement of time: for example, Irma, who never wears a watch, 'guessed with my head and knew with my heart' (p.145), whereas Mr Cutler, Colonel Fitzhubert's gardener, 'like most people who live in close daily contact with nature was aware of elemental rhythms' (p.199). Time in *Picnic at Hanging Rock* is inexorable, linear, measured – but also susceptible to pause, cyclical, elemental. Like the mystery at the heart of the novel, it defies explanation.

Key point

Joan Lindsay had a fascination with time throughout her life, and allegedly could not wear a watch without it stopping, just as the watches of various characters stop. Her fascination is evident in the title of her autobiography, *Time without Clocks*.

Class

Key quotes

'The Headmistress knew a lady when she saw one, and Mademoiselle de Poitiers was definitely a social asset on the staff, not to be easily replaced.' (p.132)

'There was no obstructive nonsense, for instance, in Mike's father being a Conservative member of the English House of Lords, while Albert's, when last heard of, was an itinerant rouse-about, in perpetual strife with the Boss of the Shed.' (p.81)

Picnic at Hanging Rock picks up a common theme in Australian writing in the idea that Australia is an egalitarian space where class distinctions are flattened and character is more important than birth. Michael Fitzhubert is the key example of Australian egalitarianism: in Australia a mere few weeks before the disappearances (p.31), he is a 'new chum' (p.85) – a naive new arrival, whose ignorance of Australian life marks the difference between the colonies and the mother country. But Michael shows an inclination to sink into the egalitarianism of Australia: he thinks of Australia as a place 'where anything might happen', as opposed to England, where 'everything had been done before, quite often by one's own ancestors, over and over again' (p.34). That Michael thinks this while sitting in the shadows of Hanging Rock is one of the central paradoxes of Australia in the novel: an ancient country that is perpetually new in possibilities. Michael leans into these possibilities, befriending Albert rather than squiring Miss Sprack from Government Cottage at his aunt's garden party (p.82), rejecting the possibility of marrying a wealthy heiress who moves in the highest social circles (p.158) and ending up on a cattle station in Northern Queensland (p.246).

But, in a sense, the novel also treats this Australian egalitarianism as illusory, presenting Michael's transformation to 'Mike' alongside a series of pairings of good servants versus bad servants. Lindsay has sometimes been said to show a fascination with pairs in the novel, and this is one such example, where those who perform admirably are rewarded and those who break from their expected roles are sometimes punished. Take the two Appleyard College servants, Minnie and Alice. Minnie is as 'dainty as a fairy about a house' (p.208) and one of the few characters to be kind to Sara, bringing her jelly and cream that she 'pinched ... off Madam's dinner tray' and setting a meal out prettily on a tray 'with a lace-trimmed cloth and Japanese china' (p.194). She is ultimately rewarded with 'unguessed-at future joys, including a comfortable cottage to be erected behind the stables at Lake View and later to be filled with merry-eyed infants the spit and image of Irish Tom' (p.209). Lindsay makes clear that this is a kind of moral reward, describing it as 'another segment of the Hanging Rock pattern' (p.209). Alice, conversely, is a 'big, blowsy girl' who Mademoiselle stigmatises as a 'blundering creature' (p.220). Alice is so 'sick and tired of the boarders and their nonsense' (p.221) that she fails to bring Sara her breakfast. Although she is not punished, nor is she rewarded, disappearing from the novel with the decision 'to get herself a job as a waitress after Easter' (p.221).

A more sustained example is the pairing of the two teachers, Mademoiselle de Poitiers and Miss Lumley, one of whom is rewarded richly and the other punished brutally. Mademoiselle is an elegant, cosmopolitan woman, kind and sympathetic to the students (although she has a clear favourite in Irma) and respectful towards her colleagues. Dora Lumley is a narrow-minded woman, fond of her brother but otherwise without strong ties of family or friendship, cowardly and given to petty tyrannies towards the students. Mademoiselle is rewarded with marriage to a man of such virtue that even Ben Hussey of the Woodend livery stables has heard of and values him (pp.26–7), and a long life with many grandchildren (p.177). Dora Lumley, conversely, burns to death in a cheap room in a Melbourne hotel with her brother, the only person for whom she has ever shown affection. It is perhaps the most brutal punishment in the novel for a character who is merely cowardly and occasionally perpetrates petty cruelties.

But the major example in the text is the differing paths of Albert Crundall and Sara Waybourne. Albert is a faithful servant. Even when he is rewarded by Irma's father, he is reluctant to leave his position until he finds Tom as a replacement because 'the old bastard's treated me pretty good, taking it all round' (p.201). Despite his friendship with Mike, Albert is conscious of status and reluctant to overstep social boundaries. This is seen most clearly in his refusal to respond to Irma's overtures of friendship (pp.153–4), even with her desire to thank him for her recovery. The reward of £1000 from Mr Leopold allows Albert to leave his position and to strike out on his own, but it is in many ways a reward for being a faithful servant: for following Mike's lead and thus saving Irma. Sara, on the other hand, is a child outside her class: 'dragged up' (p.31), as Albert puts it, in a Ballarat orphanage, she is unaware even of her exact age and is disconnected from all family. Yet she has been raised to a standard of previously unimagined luxury by her guardian, Jasper Cosgrove, a shadowy figure in the text (how does he come to adopt a young girl from a country orphanage?), but one who is 'expensively dressed' and 'left behind him in the study the tang of eau de Cologne and morocco leather' (p.134). Sara is a peripheral figure, attached only to Miranda, teased by the other girls and bullied and punished by the staff. Unlike Albert, there is no reward for her, removed from one class and barely tolerated in another; the option she (most likely) chooses is death.

DIFFERENT INTERPRETATIONS

Different interpretations arise from different responses to a text. Over time, a text will evoke a wide range of responses from its readers, who may come from various social or cultural groups and live in very different places and historical periods. Responses by critics and reviewers can be published in newspapers, journals and books, both online and in print. They can also be expressed in discussions among readers in the media, classrooms, book groups and so on. While there is no single correct reading of a text, it is important to understand that an interpretation is more than a personal opinion – it is the justification of a point of view on the text. To present an interpretation of a text based on your point of view, you must use a logical argument and support it with relevant evidence from the text.

Critical viewpoints

The most common critical interpretations of *Picnic at Hanging Rock* focus on its position as a Gothic, particularly Australian Gothic, novel. Gerry Turcotte, a significant Australian literature critic, identifies Lindsay's novel in *The Oxford History of the Novel in English* as one of the texts that 'expand the possibilities for a modern uncanny that invokes an historic past and a frightening outback present' (2017, p.206). Although the story – schoolgirls disappearing on an excursion, and the consequences for their social circle – could be set anywhere, Lindsay's decision to use Hanging Rock and its environs is what makes this a landmark Australian Gothic novel: instead of looking to crumbling Italian castles or the majesty of the European Alps, readers are encouraged to see the uncanny and the sublime in their own country, to recognise an antiquity that surpasses the ruins of European cultures and to find the elements of the Gothic in the familiar. At a point in history when Australians were just beginning to turn away from English and American texts to explore their own literature, this was a significant move. This interpretation, however, came slowly to the novel: an early review in *The Bulletin* described it as 'too light, and even at it grimmest, too sunlit to be called Gothic' (1967, p.82). Although the anonymous critic recognised that Lindsay was working in the Gothic mode, it is only retrospectively that the novel began to be understood as Australian Gothic, rather than a less effective example of the traditional Gothic.

Gothic readings of the novel range widely. Suzette Mayr sees Appleyard College as malevolent presence in the text, 'a "broken" object ... unable to fulfill its function as a proper house that shelters and protects its inhabiting "family"' (2017, p.393): without this function, the house becomes uncanny, and all but sentient, until it represents a menace akin to that of the 'enigmatic' (p.394) Hanging Rock. Sophie Masson (2016) traces similarities to the myth of the Pied Piper. Donald Barrett, conversely, ties the novel to the Greek god Pan, who gave his name to the word 'panic' and whose 'traditional haunts are mountains, sunless caves and woods' (1982, p.300): Barrett teases out Pan's traditional links not only to hysteria, but also to sleeping and dreaming, both of which permeate the novel (p.304). The novel's reliance on dreams, the supernatural and the uncanny makes it a particularly rich text for analysis, as much in its pages defies a simple explanation.

Recently, critics have also come to question how the novel addresses – or fails to address – the traditional owners of Hanging Rock and reinforces the concept of *terra nullius*. Jay Daniel Thompson, for example, touches on the novel when he ties the Australian trope of the missing child to what he calls the 'White Nation Fantasy' (2018, p.288), which marginalises Aboriginal people and migrants of non-European backgrounds (p.289). Conversely, Kathleen Steele examines how the novel treats 'Aboriginal absence in the landscape' (2010, p.47). However, this interpretation requires one to read deeply into the text in a way that may run counter to the narrative: for example, Steele acknowledges that Lindsay 'does not dwell on the deeper implications of the "black tracker"', but asserts that the disappearances of the three girls 'offer an alternative meditation on Aboriginal absence' (p.47). Steele's analysis – particularly her connection of the novel to the Gothic elements of Barbara Baynton's much earlier short stories, in *Bush Studies* (1902) – is intriguing. However, the reading of the disappearance of three white Australians as a 'meditation on Aboriginal absence' can itself be seen as an example of absence. Lindsay's novel only acknowledges Aboriginal Australia in the character of the Indigenous tracker; not only is he an extremely peripheral figure in the text (and presented as less successful at tracking than the bloodhound), but he is also the subject of a racial slur made by one of the characters (p.83). Furthermore, sections of the novel seem to actively negate an Aboriginal presence in the landscape, such as the description of the Rock showing 'absolutely no signs of any disturbance more recent than the ravages of Nature over some hundreds or thousands of years' (p.87), although the traditional owners occupied the site until the 1830s. Reading the text as an engagement with Aboriginal dispossession, then, is risky, but it is certainly possible to read it for the ways in which it does not acknowledge Aboriginal dispossession.

Two interpretations

Interpretation 1: *Picnic at Hanging Rock* could have been set in any time and have the same effect on the reader.

The heart of *Picnic at Hanging Rock* is in the relationships between the girls who go missing and the girls who miss them, and this is a story that could be told in any time. While the setting is explicitly Edwardian, the novel draws from earlier, nineteenth-century models and also presents a central tragedy that could happen at any time, even today: people continue to go missing, and those left behind continue to grieve. The 'missing person' is a trope that defies time.

The fact that Lindsay does not present a resolution to the mystery encourages us to read the story as timeless. If, as one character suggests, the girls had been abducted and sold to a Sydney brothel, we might be more inclined to read their fate as historically specific: 'such things happened now and then in Sydney when girls of respectable backgrounds disappeared without a trace' (p.131). But since they simply vanish into the landscape, their fate becomes untethered to time and space – they vanished then, but could they not also vanish now? What about slipping back into the landscape, disappearing into the ancient rock, is specific to the Edwardian period? Certainly, there are elements of the plot that are embedded in the Edwardian setting, such as Mrs Appleyard's relief at how long it will take the news to get to the families (pp.76–8). But the disappearance itself is timeless.

Because of this, the emotional core of the novel speaks to modern readers as much as it did to contemporary readers on its publication, and as much as it might have done, if such a thing could be tested, to readers in the Edwardian period. As long as the mystery is unexplained, we as readers focus on its consequences, on the devastation left behind. This is not a whodunnit or a detective mystery, but a story of the heart: it is no coincidence that, six weeks after the disappearances, after the death of Sara, Mrs Appleyard finds in Miranda's wardrobe 'those ridiculous cards … dozens of them' (p.227). The fact that they are Valentine's Day cards is particularly significant: modern readers will be familiar with the concept, which connects them to the missing girls much more strongly than the Edwardian setting separates them.

Lindsay's novel offers a richly imagined setting: an Edwardian boarding school in the Australian bush, the fluttering of white linen 'fluted like a nautilus shell' (p.43) on the Rock, the slow movement of horse and carriage, the insistence on gloves in the hot Australian summer. But the tragedy of the girls' disappearance and the devastation it leaves behind could happen to anyone, in any time.

Interpretation 2: *Picnic at Hanging Rock* depends on its historical setting for its effect on the reader.

Picnic at Hanging Rock's Edwardian setting provides the impetus for the story. Only in this environment of strict rules, gender segregation and class divides could the story unfold in the way it does. As a nineteenth-century boarding school, Appleyard College is a single-sex place of strict rules: As the signs in the corridors remind students, 'SILENCE WAS GOLDEN' (p.15), and the girls speak softly, walk in pairs and learn the social niceties that will make them fine Edwardian women – such as the propriety of blue ribbons with white muslin (p.12) – along with a smattering of English history (p.15).

Similarly, the consequences, both major and minor, of the disappearances are driven by the Edwardian setting. As a minor example, Irma's crossing of paths with Albert Crundall (p.153) is all the more dramatic for its unlikeliness in a society that separates the wealthy and the workers: Albert 'knew, with absolute certainty, that he would never speak to Irma Leopold again' (p.155). Dora and Reg Lumley's deaths in a hotel fire are possible at any time, but would they, in a modern novel, break a journey to Warragul (p.197), barely 100 kilometres from Melbourne, if they were travelling in modern conveyances? The silence of Miranda's parents on the loss of their only and beloved daughter is also unsurprising in a time when mail travels slowly, and may reach the vast isolation of a cattle station 'with the stores, sometimes only once in four or five weeks' (p.77) – time enough, in the six weeks of the novel, for a letter to arrive to the parents, but not time enough for their response.

More dramatic still is the situation of Sara Waybourne. Some seven years younger than her brother, Albert, she likely remembers little before the orphanage: certainly, although she calls out for Albert at one point in the novel (p.47), she never mentions either father or mother. Presumably intended for domestic service like her brother, she is adopted by a wealthy guardian, who seems to shower her with books, drawing instruments and clothes (pp.230–1), but with whom she otherwise has a rather distant relationship: at the time of the novel's events, in February and March, she has not had a letter from him since the previous Christmas, and seems unperturbed by this, asking only, 'I wonder why he hasn't written for such a long time? I want some books and some more crayons' (p.135). Is this relationship possible in a modern setting, or does it depend on an Edwardian model of social welfare for its plausibility?

Similarly, Sara is at the whim of Mrs Appleyard's increasingly volatile moods in a manner unlikely in a modern heroine. The final stages of the novel, with the escalating bullying, mistreatment and isolation of Sara, are some of the most affecting scenes. But they are events embedded in the Edwardian present of the text – a world where silence was golden, where girls could be starved and strapped to a backboard for posture correction (as on page 183, when Sara is not only strapped down but also forgotten). Would a modern Sara submit to this treatment? Edwardian Sara has no choice: the petty tyrannies and punishments of Appleyard College are still an improvement on the horrors of the orphanage. We see this when Mrs Appleyard, rummaging in Sara's room as Sara herself lies at the base of the tower, hears her again 'cry out, "No, no! Not that! Not the orphanage!"' (p.227). Girls in black bloomers, in blue ribbons, in white linen: *Picnic at Hanging Rock* depends on its Edwardian setting for their triumphs of valentines and picnics, but most of all for their tragedies.

QUESTIONS & ANSWERS

This section focuses on your own analytical writing on the text, and gives you strategies for producing high-quality responses in your coursework and exam essays.

An essay on a literary work is a formal and serious piece of writing that presents your point of view on the text, usually in response to a given topic. Your 'point of view' in an essay is your interpretation of the meaning of the text's language, structure, characters, situations and events, supported by detailed analysis of textual evidence.

Analyse – don't summarise

In your essays it is important to avoid simply summarising what happens in a text.

- A **summary** is a description or paraphrase (retelling in different words) of the characters and events. For example: 'Macbeth has a horrifying vision of a dagger dripping with blood before he goes to murder King Duncan.'
- An **analysis** is an explanation of the real meaning or significance that lies 'beneath' the text's words (and images, for a film). For example: 'Macbeth's vision of a bloody dagger shows how deeply uneasy he is about the violent act he is contemplating, and conveys his sense that supernatural forces are impelling him to act.'

A limited amount of summary is sometimes necessary to let your reader know which part of the text you wish to discuss. However, always keep this to a minimum and follow it immediately with your analysis of what this part of the text is really telling us.

Plan your essay

Carefully plan your essay so that you have a clear idea of what you are going to say. The plan ensures that your ideas flow logically, that your argument remains consistent and that you stay on the topic. An essay plan should be a list of **brief dot points** covering no more than half a page.

- Include your central argument or main contention – a concise statement of your overall response to the topic.
- Write three or four dot points for each paragraph, indicating the main idea and evidence/examples from the text. Note that in your essay you will need to *expand* on these points and *analyse* the evidence.

Structure your essay

An essay is a complete, self-contained piece of writing. It has a clear beginning (the introduction), middle (several body paragraphs) and end (the last paragraph or conclusion). It must also have a central argument that runs throughout, linking each paragraph to form a coherent whole. See examples of introductions and conclusions in the 'Analysing a sample topic' and 'Sample answer' sections.

The introduction establishes your overall response to the topic. It includes your main contention and outlines the main evidence you will refer to in the course of the essay. Write your introduction *after* you have done a plan and *before* you write the rest of the essay.

The body paragraphs argue your case – they present evidence from the text and explain how this evidence supports your argument. Each body paragraph needs:

- a strong **topic sentence** (usually the first sentence) that states the main point being made in the paragraph
- **evidence** from the text, including some brief quotations
- **analysis** of the textual evidence, with **explanation** of its significance and how it supports your argument
- **links back to the topic** in one or more statements, usually towards the end of the paragraph.

Connect the body paragraphs so that your discussion flows smoothly. Use some linking words and phrases such as 'similarly' and 'on the other hand', though don't start every paragraph like this. Another strategy is to use a significant word from the last sentence of one paragraph in the first sentence of the next.

Use key terms from the topic – or synonyms for them – throughout, so the relevance of your discussion to the topic is always clear.

The conclusion ties everything together and finishes the essay. It includes strong statements that emphasise your central argument and provide a clear response to the topic.

Avoid simply restating the points made earlier in the essay – this will end on a very flat note and imply that you have run out of ideas and vocabulary. The conclusion should be a logical extension of what you have written, not just a repetition or summary of it. Writing an effective conclusion can be a challenge. Try using these tips:

- Start by linking back to the final sentence of the second-last paragraph – this helps your writing to flow, rather than leaping back to your main contention straight away.
- Use synonyms and expressions with equivalent meanings to vary your vocabulary. This allows you to reinforce your line of argument without being repetitive.
- When planning your essay, think of one or two broad statements or observations about the text's wider meaning. These should be related to the topic and your overall argument. Keep them for the conclusion, since they will give you something 'new' to say but still follow logically from your discussion. The introduction will be focused on the topic, but the conclusion can present a wider view of the text.

Essay topics

1. 'Joan Lindsay demonstrates an ongoing fascination with time throughout *Picnic at Hanging Rock*.'
   What role does time play in the novel?
2. "So too have the lives of innumerable lesser fry – spiders, mice, beetles – whose scuttlings, burrowings and terrified retreats are comparable, if on a smaller scale."
   What role does the natural world play in *Picnic at Hanging Rock*?
3. How does *Picnic at Hanging Rock* present a difference between the socially constructed and the natural model of girlhood?
4. 'The Australian bush is presented as relentlessly malevolent in *Picnic at Hanging Rock*.' Discuss.
5. "Whether *Picnic at Hanging Rock* is fact or fiction, my readers must decide for themselves."
   What effect does this statement have on our reading of the novel?
6. '*Picnic at Hanging Rock* would not work as a contemporary story: it relies entirely on its historical setting for meaning.'
   To what extent is this statement true?
7. 'Despite the text's Australian setting, there is nothing specifically Australian about Lindsay's use of the Gothic in *Picnic at Hanging Rock*.' Discuss.
8. '*Picnic at Hanging Rock* successfully attempts to map the European concept of the sublime onto the Australian landscape.'
   Do you agree?
9. 'The Gothic has been called a literature of terror, of dystopia, of unsettlement.' (Turcotte 2017)
   How true is this of *Picnic at Hanging Rock*?
10. '*Picnic at Hanging Rock* is a novel of the contest between human and nature.' Discuss.

Vocabulary for writing on *Picnic at Hanging Rock*

Australian Gothic: the genre, of which *Picnic at Hanging Rock* is a key example, imposes the European Gothic onto the Australian landscape, using the classical Gothic elements of unsettling, uncanny and sinister events against the backdrop of the vast Australian landscape. In some instances, there is an undercurrent of the violence of colonialism.

Edwardian: the novel is often described as Edwardian, although it is technically very late Victorian; Edward VII succeeded his mother, Queen Victoria, in January 1901, and his official coronation was not until August 1902. Because it was followed by the devastation of the two World Wars, the Edwardian era (c.1901–10, sometimes extended to 1914) is often treated romantically, as a wealthy, optimistic social period. In Australia, it is also the early years of Federation, marking a significant change in Australian government and identity. The French refer to roughly the same period as La Belle Epoque, and Americans use the term 'the Gilded Age'.

The sublime: in literature and art, this concept refers to greatness that is beyond all possibility of calculation or imitation. It was explored in German philosophy, and to a lesser extent in English philosophy, in the eighteenth and early nineteenth centuries, and had a strong influence on the Romantic poets of the period and on Gothic fiction. The most common example of the sublime is grandiose landscapes, but it can apply to anything, from the aesthetic to the moral. Marion Quade's obsession with calculation and measurement defies the sublime.

The uncanny: although the term was not invented by Sigmund Freud, it is best known from his 1919 essay of the same name 'Das Unheimliche'. The uncanny occurs when something that should be ordinary appears strange: Freud used the example of dolls and waxworks, which appear human but are not. The term 'uncanny valley' in animation draws on this concept. Edith's experience as the girls walk away from her on the Rock is an example of the uncanny.

Analysing a sample topic

This section leads you through the analysis of a single topic and the planning of a response.

'The Australian bush is presented as relentlessly malevolent in *Picnic at Hanging Rock.*' Discuss.

This question relies on your determining whether the bush can be described as 'malevolent' and, if so, whether that malevolence is relentless. There are several possible approaches: for example, 'malevolence' generally assumes an intelligence behind it; a malevolent presence actively wishes to cause harm. It is possible to argue, then, that the bush causes harm, but not out of malevolence, since there is no intelligence behind the acts. The sample response below, however, takes a different perspective: that the bush is malevolent, but not relentlessly so. Both aspects of this argument rest on the fact that not everyone who ventures onto Hanging Rock is swallowed up.

Sample introduction

> In *Picnic at Hanging Rock*, the Australian bush is presented as malevolently drawing people away into itself, swallowing them up without a trace. This is seen most clearly in the disappearance of the schoolgirls and Miss McCraw. However, the malevolence cannot be seen as relentless, for two reasons: firstly, not everyone who is drawn into the bush disappears and, secondly, not everyone who ventures onto the Rock is swallowed up. Chief among those who do not vanish are Edith and Albert, who both spend considerable time on the Rock. Therefore, although the bush is presented as malevolent, it is a selective and not relentless evil.

Body paragraph outline

Body paragraph 1: The Australian bush is presented as malevolent, especially in the case of the missing schoolgirls.

- Use the disappearance of the schoolgirls as the basis for an argument about the malevolence of the bush.
- Remember, it is necessary to make a case for intelligent activity: the bush is not merely *dangerous* but *actively malevolent*.
- The two best examples in favour of this argument are Edith's perception that the girls are moving almost without their own volition (possibly even against their will) and Miss McCraw being drawn up from the Picnic Grounds.

Body paragraph 2: Several characters are capable of partially resisting the malevolence of the bush.

- The best example of this is Michael Fitzhubert, particularly in Chapters 7 and 8. Use examples – such as his hallucination of Miranda or the strange note left for Albert – that suggest that, like the girls, Michael is acting almost outside his own volition.
- Unlike the girls, however, Michael can be seen as struggling against the bush's malevolence: the note, with its strange syntax, can be read as an attempt to break free of some influence to leave traces for others to follow.
- Michael is found, rather than vanishing; although Irma is also found, none of the others are, and some trace should have been evident.

Body paragraph 3: The fact that not everyone is swallowed up offers evidence that the bush is not relentlessly malevolent.

- Five people (the girls, Miss McCraw and Michael) are seen as strongly affected by what appears to be an active, malevolent landscape.
- Not everyone in the novel is affected. Lesser characters are indicative of this: Colonel and Mrs Fitzhubert, Constable Grant, Doctor Cooling and all the members of the search parties are seemingly immune, as well as various unnamed characters, such as the rabbiters in the final chapter.

Body paragraph 4: The fates of Edith and Albert offer evidence that the Rock itself is not relentlessly malevolent.

- Edith is in the immediate presence of the girls when they disappear but seems almost entirely unaffected (although she does indicate a degree of memory loss, like Irma).
- Albert spends a long period searching for Michael and is likewise not shown as responding to any malevolent force. Unlike Edith, he does not even seem mildly affected.
- Were the Rock relentlessly malevolent, Edith and Albert would be affected.

Sample conclusion

> If the Australian bush in *Picnic at Hanging Rock* is malevolent, as it appears to be, it is not a relentlessly malevolent force. The bush has the means of drawing people into itself, almost against their will: it draws not only the schoolgirls, who are climbing the Rock, but also Miss McCraw, who is in the Picnic Grounds at its base. However, this malevolent activity is not entirely relentless: characters are capable of resisting the bush's draw, as Michael Fitzhubert manages to do, and some characters are completely unaffected. Chief among the latter are Edith Horton, who is present when the girls disappear but, barring her panic, is not affected, and Michael's companion, Albert Crundall. Therefore, although there is a malevolence to the bush in *Picnic at Hanging Rock*, it is presented as selective rather than relentless.

SAMPLE ANSWER

How does *Picnic at Hanging Rock* present a difference between the socially constructed and the natural model of girlhood?

Throughout *Picnic at Hanging Rock*, the idea of natural (particularly Australian) girlhood competes with the socially constructed model of young women that Appleyard College seeks to create. Miranda is the one character who successfully embodies both aspects, as a natural Australian girl and a socially accomplished young woman. More common is the model of Edith, to whom nature is alien, while Sara Waybourne represents a character who cannot be moulded as Appleyard College wishes. The contrast between the natural state and the constructed model of girlhood is most graphically represented in the scene of hysteria in the gymnasium.

Just as Appleyard College is out of place in the Australian landscape, so too are the students out of place at Hanging Rock, dressed in Edwardian summer linen, corsets, drawers, stockings and gloves. The novel consciously plays with this disconnect between nature and society through the characters of the students. Of all the students, only Miranda is able to straddle both: as her parents recall, she can both ride a horse and command a drawing room; she opens gates easily and moves comfortably through the bush, and yet is also an accomplished and popular head girl. Remembered as a 'tall pale girl' or a swan (and sometimes, as in Michael's vision, both), she represents the possibility of natural and constructed girlhood co-existing.

But Miranda is an exception. Most students are closer to the model offered by Edith Horton. Edith consistently refutes any connection to the natural world, not realising that horses have grandmothers, or understanding why people choose to live in the country, and complaining vociferously on the climb up the Rock. But Edith's resistance to nature is itself not natural, but socially constructed. As she indicates when she says she is not learning mathematics, her mother has a particular idea of what is and is not suitable for young women, and institutions such as Appleyard College help shape what could otherwise be natural girls into these social models. Perhaps her blunted sensitivity to the natural world is why Edith does not disappear on the Rock with the others.

Conversely, Sara Waybourne is a character with an affinity to the natural world, but she is not as sculptable as Edith. Sara is commonly affiliated with pansies: she begs them from the gardener for her room at the College, and when she appears to her brother, she is announced by the scent of pansies. She dies, fittingly, among the hydrangeas, which are one of the earliest motifs in the book. She also sympathises with Miranda's affinity for nature, refusing to colour her black-and-white photograph of Miranda because Miranda refused to have her naturally straight hair curled for the picture. Yet her story is one of people trying and failing to mould her into the social norm of girlhood: she cannot learn poems by heart as the other girls do, and the 'backboard' that is designed to give her suitable posture is actually used as a punishment. Even her guardian is not entirely sure of how to dress her as a young woman. Sara's tragedy is that she cannot transcend nature and society as Miranda does.

The most striking example of natural and social models of girlhood clashing is in the scene with Irma in the gymnasium. The gymnasium is where the girls are shaped into socially acceptable women: the backboard is kept there, and deportment exercises are carried out there too. But when Irma visits, the natural and the social collide: instead of seeing the gymnasium, the girls hallucinate the Picnic Grounds and the shadow of the Rock, and the sight brings on a mass hysteria akin to Edith's panic at the Rock. Indeed, Edith, the prime example of the social model of girlhood, is the ringleader of the panicking girls. The hysteria is dispersed, but its memory lingers for years. Just as the college is ultimately destroyed by bushfire, this scene suggests that the socially constructed person will always be weaker than nature.

Picnic at Hanging Rock puts the natural model of girlhood in tension with social ideas of suitable behaviour from the moment the girls strip off their gloves and beg to remove their hats. With the exception of Miranda, who effortlessly straddles both social mores and natural life, the girls are either stripped of their natural instincts (like Edith) or destroyed by attempts to bring them into social patterns of behaviour (like Sara). The novel suggests that social patterns of behaviour can always be unbalanced by nature.

REFERENCES & READING

Text

Lindsay, J 2019, *Picnic at Hanging Rock*, Text Publishing, Melbourne. First published 1967.

References

Barrett, D 1982, 'The Mythology of Pan and *Picnic at Hanging Rock*', *Southerly*, vol. 42, no. 3, pp.299–308.

Masson, S 2016, 'Fairy Tale Transformation: The Pied Piper Theme in Australian Fiction', *M/C Journal*, vol. 16, no. 4, http://journal.media-culture.org.au/index.php/mcjournal/article/view/1116

Mayr, S 2017, '"Misfit" College: The Sentient House as Thing in Joan Lindsay's *Picnic at Hanging Rock*', *Antipodes*, vol. 31, no. 2, pp.393–406.

McCulloch, J 2017, *Beyond the Rock: The Life of Joan Lindsay and the Mystery of* Picnic at Hanging Rock, Bonnier Publishing, Richmond.

Reuschmann, E 2004, 'Out of Place: Reading (Post) Colonial Landscapes as Gothic Space in Jane Campion's Films', *Post Script*, vol. 24, no. 2–3, pp.8–21.

Rousseau, Y 1980, *The Murders at Hanging Rock*, Scribe, Fitzroy.

Steele, K 2010, 'Fear and Loathing in the Australian Bush: Gothic Landscapes in *Bush Studies* and *Picnic at Hanging Rock*', *Colloquy*, no. 20, pp. 33–56.

The Bulletin 1967, 'Sunlit Mystery', vol. 89, no. 4579, p.82.

Thompson, JD 2018, 'The Country of Sexualised Children: Whiteness, Innocence, and the "Sexualisation of Childhood"', *Journal of Australian Studies*, vol. 42, no. 3, pp.285–96.

Turcotte, G 2017, 'Postcolonial Gothic', in CA Howells et al. (eds), *The Oxford History of the Novel in English: Volume 12*, Oxford University Press, Oxford, pp.205–20.

Whittaker, A 2017, 'Many Girls White Linen', *Overland*, no. 226, pp.29–30.

Further reading/viewing

Cook, K 1961, *Wake in Fright*, Michael Joseph, London.

Cusack, D and James, F 1951, *Come In Spinner*, Heinemann, Melbourne.

Johnston, G 1964, *My Brother Jack*, Collins, London.

Marshall, JV 1959, *Walkabout*, Michael Joseph, London.

Shelley, M 1818, *Frankenstein*, Lackington, Hughes, Harding, Mavor, & Jones, London.

Shute, N 1950, *A Town Like Alice*, Heinemann, London.

Stevenson, RL 1886, *Strange Case of Dr Jekyll and Mr Hyde*, Longman, Green & Co., London.

Stoker, B 1897, *Dracula*, Archibald Constable & Co., London.

Stow, R 1958, *To the Islands*, McDonald, London.

Terror Nullius 2018, dir. Dominique and Dan Angeloro [Soda_Jerk], Australian Centre for the Moving Image.

Wake in Fright 1971, dir. Ted Kotcheff, Group W Films. Starring Gary Bond, Chips Rafferty, and Donald Pleasance.

Walkabout 1971, dir. Nicholas Roeg, Max L. Raab – Si Litvinoff Film Productions. Starring Jenny Agutter, David Gulpilil, and Luc Roeg.

Walpole, H 1764, *Castle of Otranto*, William Bathoe, London.

White, P 1957, *Voss*, Eyre & Spottiswood, London.